Wannabe Guide to

WINE

Wannabe Guide to

WINE

by

JACK MINGO

RDR Books
Berkeley, California

RDR Books
PO Box 5212
Berkeley, California 94705

ISBN: 1-57143-039-3
Library of Congress Card Catalog Number: 95-72162

Cover Image: Michael Tofanelli / Stock Illustration Source
Cover Design: Bonnie Smetts Design
Book Design: Paula Morrison
Illustrations: Sergei Ponomarov

Printed in Hong Kong by Twin Age Limited

Contents

Why Learn about Wine?

Is wine an elixir of life ... or just a drink made from rotten grapes that makes you high? Do wine snobs really know something you don't ... or are they just faking as a way of impressing everybody?

Actually it doesn't matter. Learning about wine has little or nothing to do with the beverage. Learning about wine has to do with being at ease in awkward situations. Learning about wine means having control over whether the people around you feel at ease or uncomfortable in those same situations.

Take yourself for example: Did you get this book to better fulfill your life and give yourself a broader understanding of the whole *gestalt* that goes into the mystery of wine? Did you get it to learn how to better enjoy the experience of drinking wine?

Yeah, right. Tell us another one.

No, you got the *Wannabe Guide to Wine* for one or more of the following reasons:

1. You have an obnoxious friend, co-worker, relative, spouse, or neighbor who is always lording it over you about how much he (it is usually a he) knows about wine. You wonder if maybe you can either get the same smug self-assurance, or put that person in his or her place, by also learning about wines.

2. You feel like a fool whenever confronted with a wine moment of truth. Every wine decision becomes a wine crisis. You go to a restaurant and the waiter asks *you* which wine you want. You have no idea why he's handing you the cork, but the last time—when you sniffed, licked, and bit off its end—he gave you a funny look. You go to a store to buy a bottle for a good dinner and spend forty-five minutes agonizing: What will go with the main dish? If "red with red meat" is the rule why did that sweet red you bought the last time make the beef taste like mildew?

3. You're pretty sure that learning about wines will transform you from being a whimpering little nebbish into a sophisticate with flair and élan. You want to impress friends and potential, present, or former sexual partners with your style, class, and knowledge.

4. Your potential, present, or former sexual partner bought this for you in the hope that you'll finally *develop* some style, class, and knowledge.

5. You want to be thought of as a bigshot wine expert who can even pronounce Sauvignon Blanc, Gewürztraminer, and *Appellations d'origine contrôlée* without stumbling. You hope to bully and dominate the people around you by playing on *their* insecurities for a change, ha ha ha ha HA!

That's power. And it's yours with the *Wannabe Guide to Wine*. Use it wisely.

A Short Wine History

*"The peoples of the Mediterranean began to emerge from
barbarism when they learnt to cultivate the olive and the
grape vine."*
     —Thucydides, fifth-century B.C. Greek historian

When did wine first appear on the earth? If you believe the
Bible, Noah was the first winemaker, after the flood. Wine
was important in Biblical times: In the whole of the Old Tes-
tament, only the book of Jonah has no reference to it. Isa-
iah even includes advice on how to plant a vineyard. (For
more biblical wine lore, see page 53.)

According to Omar Khayyám, the first person to discover
wine was a member of a Persian king's harem. Khayyám's
story has it that grapes were stored in jars in the king's palace
for eating out of season. One jar developed a strange smell
and foaming grapes; it was set aside as probably poisonous.
A member of the harem, suffering from "nervous headaches,"
decided to use this "poison" to commit suicide and free her-
self from the constant pain. Instead, her headache disap-
peared, she became the life of the party, and then sank into
a restful sleep.

According to historian Hugh Johnson, though, wine was
probably the first alcoholic drink. The idea makes sense.
Unlike beer, which has to be actively fermented, wine did

not have to be invented: it would happen any time grapes or any other fruit were stored a little too long. Johnson thinks that wine was likely discovered at least two million years ago.

Soviet archeologists have found evidence of the transition from wild grapevines to cultivated ones sometime during the Stone Age, about 7000–5000 B.C. However, the earliest solid archaeological evidence of wine—a jar with wine residues found in Mesopotamia—has been dated roughly to 3500 B.C. Mesopotamia's earliest wine is believed to have been made from dates (which seems appropriate, since people have been using wine to "make their dates" ever since).

Egyptian wall paintings from 3,000–5,000 years ago show that the technology of winemaking has not changed much since then. Wine was important to the Egyptians—King Tut was buried with thirty-six jars of it to help him make a smooth transition to the Next World.

According to Homer, Odysseus took wine from his own island of Ithaca on his trip to Troy. But he also got some high octane wine, perhaps a distilled spirit, as a ransom from Mara, a priest of Apollo in Thrace. This "honey sweet red wine," so strong that it was usually mixed with water in a 1:20 dilution, was what put the Cyclops into a stupor so Odysseus could poke out its eye.

Not all ancient wine techniques were good ones. There has been quite a bit of controversy about sulfites in wine in recent times. Even though the earliest known documentation goes back to 1487 when a royal decree in Germany legalized the practice, historians claim that the practice of adding burnt sulfur to wine as a preservative goes back thousands of years.

Another bad idea—the Romans discovered that they could "sweeten" their wine with lead. Lead poisoning is believed to be one of the causes of the fall of the Roman Empire, yet even after Dr. Eberhard Gockel of Germany discovered that lead was a deadly, cumulative poison in 1696, the practice of using lead in wine was not banned in most countries until the mid-1800s. (Even this didn't stop French winemakers who, as late as 1884, continued surreptitiously to drop lead musket balls into their barrels of wine.)

Romans drank their wine diluted with warm water. Many preferred the salty tang of sea water to the blandness of fresh water. *"It has a fishy nose, with flavors of tentacles and fins...."*

In Rome during the second century B.C., women were forbidden to drink wine. A husband who discovered his wife soaking up the Sauvignon was allowed to divorce or even kill her with impunity.

The worship of Bacchus, the wine god, was a serious religion that was suppressed in 186 B.C., but it continued in secret until its popularity led Julius Caesar to lift the ban. Mark Anthony was a practicing member. Bacchanalia was its major holiday, which was eventually usurped as Christmas by the Christians. Other elements borrowed by the new Christian cult: Bacchus's halo as a symbol of divinity, and eating bread and wine to symbolically ingest the body and blood of the god (in fact, Bacchus's blood *was* wine). Other parallels: Bacchus was the son of a god and a mortal woman and he worked miracles. Eventually, the new cult supplanted the old cult in Rome. The Christians learned a lesson from the earlier, unsuccessful attempts to suppress them—when they got a chance, they did it right. The followers of Bacchus were persecuted to the point of extinction.

Before the French got the hang of making wine, around 200 B.C., they used to buy wine from the wily Italians, exchanging a French slave for every large amphora of wine.

Jesus's first miracle was reportedly turning water into wine. He referred to wine often, calling himself "the true vine," and used wine in the Last Supper. He even talked of humanity in grape grower terms: "Every bunch in me that beareth not fruit he taketh away; and every branch that beareth fruit, he purgeth it, that it may bring forth more fruit."

The proper use of wine in Christian ceremony, like a lot of other apparently trivial things, has even set off century-long doctrinal disputes. In the Greek church in the twelfth century, the Greeks and Armenians split over whether the Eucharist wine should be watered, with the Armenians refusing to water their wine and the Greeks insisting that it was a spiritual necessity. The Armenians offered a compromise in 1178—they would add water as long as it didn't have to be warm water as demanded by the Greeks. The Greeks refused to budge. Finally, a Muslim was brought in as a neutral arbiter. After listening to both sides, he issued his opinion: Since wine itself was an impure liquid forbidden by the Koran, they should skip the wine and serve the water, either hot or cold. Both sides rejected his advice.

Wine had been banned by the Muslim clerics years earlier, to the great despair of the Arabic doctors, then among the best in the world. They used wine as medicine and as a disinfectant. The ban on wine was a result of statements like this from Mohammed, quoted in the Koran: "Believers, wine and games of chance, idols and divining arrows, are abominations devised by Satan. Avoid them, so that you may prosper. Satan seeks to stir up enmity and hatred among you by means of wine and gambling, and to keep you from the remembrance of Allah and from your prayers. Will you not abstain from them?"

During his lifetime, Mohammed enforced his request, above, with forty lashes to any who was caught violating it. His successor doubled that, equaling the penalty for violating maidens on the grounds that drinking wine inevitably leads to such things anyway.

Not all Muslims followed the injunction, of course. Even Mohammed's favorite wife (he had seven) quoted him as saying, "You may drink, but do not get drunk," while quaffing his *nabidh*, a wine made from dates. Other Islamic wine drinkers justified their drinking with another Koranic verse: "No blame shall be attached to those that have embraced the faith and done good works in regard to any food they may have eaten, so long as they fear Allah, believe in him, and do good works."

Leif Ericson, who landed in America in 1000 A.D., named the new continent Vinland the Good, based on his impression that the continent was completely covered in grapevines. He made two voyages and started a settlement, possibly near Cape Cod, where some historians believe that the first "amusing little domestic wine" was made.

Nondrinking can be a sign of fanaticism, believed King Louis XVI. In his last letter before he lost his head in the French Revolution, King Louis blamed the political savagery of the revolutionaries on the fact that its leader Robespierre drank only water, not wine.

Louis Pasteur first developed pasteurization in the 1850s as a way to prevent the spoiling of wine. Afterward, he realized it could also be used on other substances like milk. Pasteurization came just in time. When the Prussians laid Paris under siege in the winter of 1870, there was little in the way of food in the city, but plenty of wine. One famous restaurant, Voisin, provided exactly one menu item for Christmas Day: *"Chat flanqué de rats, accompagné d'un Bollinger frappé."*

Meanwhile, in America, the wine trade had already begun thriving half a century earlier on both coasts. Most people nowadays think that California wine is a relatively recent phenomenon, as if the Gallo Brothers came over a ridge, saw a vision, and started an industry earlier in this century. However, both Napa and Sonoma wineries came from a completely different set of "brothers"—Franciscan monks, who in 1824 started growing grapes and making wine at the Solano Mission in Sonoma. The wine industry they began continues to the present, interrupted only by Prohibition early in this century.

Oddly, the first large-scale American winegrowing region was not on either coast, but in Cincinnati, Ohio, of all places. In the 1850s it was known as "The Rhine of America." In 1870, America's largest winery was located on Middle Bass Island, just off the grape-growing town of Sandusky, Ohio.

How Is Wine Made, Anyway?

Wine is easy to make. You don't even have to take off your shoes and stomp grapes. In fact, you don't have to do much—just leave a bunch of grape juice lying around uncovered, and in a few weeks you'll have wine . . . of sorts.

Here's how it works. Grape juice has sugar in it. Over time, yeasts in the air settle in and start eating the sugar. Multiplying rapidly (given the right conditions, they can double their population every two hours), the yeasts change the sugar to alcohol and carbon dioxide gas. If you let the gas escape in an open vat, you get wine. If you trap it, you get bubbly wine (called "sparkling wine" in the jargon) like Champagne.

As I say, this will give you wine . . . of sorts. Making good wine, however, takes a few more steps. To quote oenologist Roger Boulton of the University of California at Davis, "Ninety percent of winemaking has nothing to do with the wine-maker. All a winemaker is doing is preventing spoilage, introducing style characteristics, and bottling it."

Here are the steps winemakers go through: First they crush the newly-harvested grapes to rupture the skins which otherwise, when unbroken, act as a barricade to repel the yeasts. The sticky mass of skins, pulp, and juice goes into a vat, where the winemaker often adds sulfur (the "sulfites" that are now mentioned on the label to warn people with allergies) to inhibit the wild yeasts in the air. The winemaker then adds a dose of tame, friendly, domestic yeasts, the kind that come eagerly when you call their name and like to curl up at the foot of the wine master after a long, hard day of fermentation and asexual mitosis.

The friendly, eager-to-please yeast immediately goes to work, bubbling and frothing the grapey mass as it releases alcohol and enough carbon dioxide to kill somebody if the vat is not properly ventilated.

Different yeasts are sensitive to different levels of alcohol. The first batch that takes over is a species called *Saccharomyces cerevisiae* that works like crazy, but gives its life for its master like Ol' Shemp when the alcohol content reaches about fourteen percent. Some wines stop fermenting at that point. But if the grapes have a high percentage of sugar (Sauternes, for example) a meaner, tougher, pit bull kind of yeast takes over at that point, called *Saccharomyces bayanus,* bringing the alcohol content even higher before it also passes on to yeast heaven.

After the yeast has fermented itself to death, you have wine. But what kind? A cloudy, chewy wine full of bits of grape pulp and skin, the carcasses of dead yeast cells, and other stuff you don't want to even know about. To settle out and extract the residue, winemakers begin "racking," a slow process of getting the solid wastes to separate from the liquid. The wine sits in a vat for a long period of time until heavier stuff slowly sinks to the bottom, at which point the winemaker siphons the wine on top into another vat. This is repeated four to eight times until the wine becomes clear and shiny. The whole process can take up to two years.

Some winemakers then filter or centrifuge the wine to get rid of the last of the microscopic yeast cells. Some connoisseurs say this also filters out some of the flavor, however, so certain winemakers do this only with "tougher" wines like Cabernet Sauvignons and Zinfandels, or not at all.

Finally, the wine is bottled, corked, labeled, and shipped off to your local wine store. (The process for sparkling wines is somewhat different. See page 39.)

Wine by Foot

"At the beginning, the product of the vine is trodden with mortal feet. Afterwards, it is served at the table of kings."
—The Talmud

You've seen it in old paintings, Disney's *Fantasia,* and that classic *I Love Lucy* episode where Lucy turns purple after a brawl in an Italian treading vat. But do winemakers really crush grapes with their feet?

Well, they used to, but they don't much any more. Foot treading is now just a historical footnote, as it were, being used with only a small quantity of the best port wine. The rest are pressed by machines which are both soulless and soleless.

That's probably just as well, because stomping grapes is harder than you'd think. For example, keeping your footing is difficult because the grape mass gets really slippery. Ancient Egyptians even invented a grid of overhead bars for treaders to hold on to because they kept falling in and drowning. (After all, a little body is considered a good thing in a wine, but an adult-sized body is not.) Today, wine treaders making port in Portugal keep from falling in by linking their arms around their neighbors' waists in a tightly-linked chain that, except for a dearth of high kicking, looks like a chorus line.

Drowning isn't the only potential danger. Over long days

and nights of treading, grapes start to ferment, releasing large enough quantities of carbon dioxide that treaders sometimes died from asphyxiation.

Despite the hazards, treading a summer's grape harvest still sort of sounds like fun to many people. However, listen to this description of a visit to a Spanish winery in 1877: "The treaders, with their white breeches well tucked up ... form three separate rows of ten men each ... and placing their arms on each other's shoulders, commence work by raising and lowering their feet ... varying this, after a time, with songs and shoutings in order to keep the weaker and the lazier ones up to the work, which is quite irksome and monotonous.... Taking part with them in the treading is a little band of musicians ... who strike up a lively tune.... The grapes become pretty well crushed and walking over the pips and stalks, strewn at the bottom of the lager, becomes something like the pilgrimages of old when the devout trudged wearily along, with hard peas backed between their feet and the soles of their shoes. The treaders move slowly in a listless way.... The fiddle strikes up anew, and the overseers drowsily upbraid. But all to no purpose. Music has lost its inspiration and authority its terrors, and the men, dead beat, raise one purple leg languidly after the other."

In Burgundy, a visiting American winegrower described this scene in the late 1800s: "Ten men, stripped of all their clothes, step into the vessel, and begin to tread down the floating mass, working it also with their hands. This operation is repeated several times if the wine does not ferment rapidly enough. The reason ... is that the bodily heat of the men aids the wine in its fermentation."

The American later declined his host's offer of a glass of red wine, choosing an untreaded white instead.

Wine Wisdom

There's something about wine that loosens the tongue and brings on loquaciousness. Some of the greatest minds of all time have given us advice about wine. Jefferson's belief that wine cures drunkenness notwithstanding, some of it even makes sense.

"Boys under eighteen should not taste wine at all, for one should not conduct fire to fire. Wine in moderation may be tasted until one is thirty years old, but the young man should abstain entirely from drunkenness and excessive drinking. But when a man is entering his fortieth year, he may summon the other gods and particularly call upon Dionysus to join the old men's holy rite, and their mirth as well, which the god has given to men to lighten their burden—wine, that is, the cure for the crabbiness of old age, whereby we may renew our youth and enjoy forgetfulness of despair."

—Plato (?427–?347 B.C.)

"Three bowls do I mix for the temperate: one to health, which they empty first, the second to love and pleasure, the third to sleep. When this bowl is drunk up, wise guests go home. The fourth bowl is ours no longer, but belongs to violence; the fifth, to uproar; the sixth to drunken revel; the seventh to black eyes; the eighth is the policeman's; the ninth belongs to biliousness; and the tenth to madness and hurling the furniture."

—Ebulus (fifth-century B.C. Greek comic playwright)

"Wine moistens and tempers the spirits, and lulls the cares of the mind to rest.... It revives our joys, and is oil to the dying flame of life. If we drink temperately, and small draughts at a time, the wine distills into our lungs like sweetest morning dew.... It is then the wine commits no rape upon our reason, but pleasantly invites us to agreeable mirth."

—Socrates (?470–399 B.C.)

"For when the wine is in, the wit is out."

—Thomas Becon (1512–1567), *Catechism*

"Lords are lordliest in their wine."

—John Milton (1608–1674), *Samson Agonistes*

"I rejoice, as a moralist, at the prospect of a reduction of the duties on wine by our legislature.... No nation is drunken where wine is cheap; and none sober, where the dearness of wine substitutes ardent spirits as the common beverage. It is, in truth, the only antidote to the bane of whiskey."

—Thomas Jefferson (1743–1826)

How to Say Wine Names

There are a lot of different kinds of wine, but not as many as you would think from all the fuss that's made over it. The hardest part is remembering how to say those names correctly, because most of them are in French. If you took a French course in school, maybe you're okay. But probably not.

Most Americans can't normally do a French accent correctly. There are two reasons for this. One is that American English is very efficient—it requires minimal mouth movement, mostly involving the lower jaw. French, on the other hand, requires a great deal of mouth contortion, particularly in the lips and upper part of the mouth.

The other reason is Maurice Chevalier. Most Americans think of him, or one of his more recent imitators, when they try to do a French accent: "Thank heav'n for leetle guhrls" and all that. That's a mistake. Maurice Chevalier is an anomaly—one of the few people on any continent who is physiologically blessed with the ability to smile while speaking with a French accent. When Americans try doing the same, it is *le disastre*.

A good French accent is (literally) foreign to Americans. It requires that you contort your lower face in a way that precludes smiling. Attitude is part of it—to get both the right facial contortion and the right attitude, think of sneering with both sides of your face as you speak, talking as if you are brimming over with anger and contempt. Purse your lips on vowels as if you've seen something that disgusts you. Make the sound come out right under your top teeth instead of right above your lower teeth. Go nasal on any "n" sounds. Try these practice phrases:

- "The food you eat in thees couhntry—Mon dieu, eet eez feet for peegs!"

- "EuroDeesney! I speet ahn your bourgeois EuroDeesney! Eet ees for l'eediot!"

- "Le cinema Americain, eet ees 'opeless, *mon ami*. A geenius like Jerry Lewis ees ground undair zee 'eel of zee 'Ollywood aristocracy. I speet on 'Ollywood!"

Okay, got it? Remember to keep that contemptuous attitude and sneering facial contortion as you practice pronouncing this list of wines. If it helps, pretend you are a snotty French maître d'. (This list is just for practice—for a more comprehensive guide to the pronunciations of individual wines, see the next chapter.)

Gamay Beaujolais (ga-may bo-zho-LAY)

Petite Sirah (pe-TEET sih-RAH)

Pinot Noir (PEE-no nwahr)

Sauvignon Blanc (so-veen-YAWHN blawhn)

Sèmillon (SEM-ee-yawhn)

Colombard (CO-lawhm-bahr)

Fumé Blanc (FEW-may blawhn)

Chenin Blanc (SHEN-nin blawhn)

Cabernet Sauvignon (ca-ber-NAY so-veen-YAWHN)

Types of Wine

"Botticelli isn't a wine, you Juggins! Botticelli's a cheese!"
—*Punch Almanac*, vol. CVI, 1894

To a lot of people, the fact that there are different kinds ("varietals") of wine is irrelevant. To the new taster, they all more or less taste like ... well, like wine. Some is kind of sweet, some is kind of sour, but it all more or less tastes like the same thing.

It is possible to develop a more refined taste. Best of all, it's also possible to *fake* having developed a more refined taste. Luckily, the various varietals of wines come with labels, so if you can read, you can have an idea of what to expect, what to taste for, and—most importantly—the words to say when all you can taste is sweet or sour.

Why are there different wine varietals? It mostly depends on what kind of grapes are used in the wine, but also can depend on how they're treated (how long the grape skins are left in during the fermentation, for example). There are at least 5,000 grape varietals which could be a nightmare to keep track of, except only about 150 of these are planted commercially, and only about a dozen produce high-quality wine nearly everywhere they're grown.

WHITE WINES

Chardonnay *(shar-doe-NAY):* Chardonnay is usually fermented in wood barrels and it is always quite "dry" (sour). It's one of the few white wines that's improved by aging. Chardonnays are sometimes described in wine talk as "bosomy." Bosomy? Experts define it as "full-bodied," if that helps. (It doesn't, of course.) They also say that Chardonnays have flavors of "butterscotch, custard, lemons, melons, hazel nuts, vanilla, green apples, tropical fruit, butter, and toast."

Fruit? Butter? Toast? Sounds like a good breakfast wine. In fact, if you find a Chardonnay that is particularly "full-bodied" and "bosomy" ... you may want to have breakfast in bed.

Serve with: Fish, shellfish, cheese (preferably not the kind from an aerosol can) and lightly seasoned poultry. That's *lightly* seasoned; if your chicken comes pre-cooked in a box with eleven secret herbs and spices, however, try something stronger like a Gewürztraminer, Cabernet, or Merlot.

Chenin Blanc *(SHEN-nin blawhn):* This is a mellow, easy to drink wine often described as "soft, round, and fruity." (A description that could fit some of the wine snobs I know as well.) When you drink and describe it, think of your supermarket's produce department, with flavorings of pears, apricots, melons, red apples, cherries, peaches, and even (as one expert put it) "canned fruit cocktail."

Serve with: Subtle to mildly spicy flavors, especially steamed or sautéed fish, even turkey sandwiches on white bread (hold the onions).

Sauvignon Blanc *(so-veen-YAWHN blawhn):* Often billed as "wild, crisp, and complex." If you need to describe it, think of camping out, because experts insist they can taste grass, wild flowers, weeds, meadow, forest, oak, eucalyptus, wild berries, mints, herbs, cedar, and smoke. With a description like this, it's hard to know whether to drink it ... or splash it on after shaving.

Serve with: Mild, unspiced fish (it is a little too much to be served with anything made by Mrs. Paul, however—not even her fish sticks), poultry, or "the other white meat," pork.

Fumé Blanc *(FEW-may blawhn):* Back in the early 1970s, California winemakers found that consumers weren't buying their Sauvignon Blancs, so they reformulated. In processing, they played down the fruity tastes, turned up the smoky ones, and called the wine Fumé Blanc—literally "white smoke." The marketing ploy worked. The wine is essentially the same as the Sauvignon Blanc, with "flinty" and "gunsmoke" tastes accentuated. Some wine experts say, without disapproval, that both wines should taste a little like "cat piss." How they'd know what that tastes like, I don't even want to speculate.

Serve with: Same as Sauvignon Blanc. Might also be good with any of the fish flavors of Little Friskies or Nine Lives.

French Colombard *(CO-lawhm-bahr):* Colombard or *Colombar* is grown primarily in the Cognac region of France, where it's considered a rather ordinary proletariat wine. It is usually fermented to a point of tart dryness, producing a wine that ranges in color through all the hues you expect to see in a good, healthy, urine sample.

Serve with: Lightly spiced fish, shellfish, and pasta. Because

it is so dry already, do not serve with acidic food ... unless you're off on a real acid trip, man. Don't serve with spicy dishes because they will beat the wimpy tastes of Colombard into submission.

Johannisberg Riesling *(REES-ling):* Some experts consider this the "most noble" white wine variety. At the very least, Riesling is to Germany as Chardonnay is to France: The classic German white wine (named after the town in Germany, not, as some suppose, the city with a similar name in South Africa). Fruitier, less nut-like than its French counterpart, the Germans sometimes leave a little residual sugar in the fermentation process to allow varying degrees of dryness (or in the jargon, it can be "bone-dry, off-dry, sweet" or anywhere in-between). Even when bone-dry, it doesn't have the jarring acidity of most whites. Descriptive words often include a whole fruit stand of sweet and juicy flavors like peaches, melons, or apricots, and sweet flowers such as honeysuckle and petunias.

Serve with: Moderately seasoned fish and shellfish. However, its balance also makes it versatile with a number of foods.

Grey Riesling *(REES-ling):* Despite the name, Grey Riesling has as much connection with Johannisberg Riesling as a hog has to do with a hogshead. It isn't even German; it's French. (Perhaps the name confusion is France's revenge for all that unpleasantness during World War II.) Most experts consider it a rather ordinary wine—more blue-collar than blue blood. Its flavor is spicy rather than fruity like a true Riesling.

Serve with: Cheez-wiz and crackers, if the wine snobs are to be believed. Actually, it's not that bad; it's just that they like to punish it for having pretensions. Try it with moderately seasoned poultry and pasta.

Gewürztraminer *(ge-vurts-tra-MEE-ner):* Gewürztraminer comes with its own built-in sobriety test: If you can't say its name, you're too drunk to have any more.

This is another genetically superior German wine: Its name means "master race." No, just kidding, Gewürz means "spicy" in German. A good glass of the "'Würz" is both fruity and spicy, and some of the words used to describe it will be reminiscent of the ingredients in a gingersnap cookie recipe: ginger, cinnamon, nutmeg, and cloves.

Serve with: Quite a few things work well with Gewürztraminer. It's not a bad wine in a restaurant when people at the table have all ordered something different. It's often good with poultry, fish in heavier sauces, and lightly seasoned pork.

Sèmillon *(SEM-ee-yawhn):* Describing this wine's taste as "broad and lanolin soft" or "refreshing but bland," experts say that the flavor components in Sèmillon include flowers, vanilla, lemon, and (ready for this?) "cotton sheets." So if you're in the habit of sampling the dust rag after using Lemon Pledge, this just might be the wine you're looking for. Some vineyards mix in a little, or a lot, of Sauvignon Blanc to give the flavor a little more character; some let you know that by calling the result "Sauterne," as in "One good sauterne deserves another." Bordeaux whites are often made of this mix as well.

Serve with: While not on a lot of restaurant wine lists, Sèmillon's not bad with mild fish and shellfish. Also if you crave lemon and cotton while doing housework, Sèmillon is probably healthier than tippling the Lemon Pledge.

Other Whites: Sylvander *(sil-VAN-der)* is kind of a wimpy Chenin Blanc; **Folle Blanche** *(fawl blahnch)* is a dry wine; **Green Hungarian** is sometimes described as undistinguished and "flaccid"; and **Muscat** *(musk-at)* tastes like raisins, not surprisingly, since raisins are also made of this grape. In the *vino del cheapo* class, you may find certain California wines in boxes and jugs with misleading generic French names like **chablis, rhine,** and **riesling.** Then there are a number of minor varietals like **Viognier, Marsanne,** and **Rousanne** that are used in blends to enhance or tone down other grapes with more personality.

RED WINES

Cabernet Sauvignon *(ca-ber-NAY so-veen-YAWHN)*: This is the Chardonnay of red wines, as it were, the pre-eminent one of its kind. Of all varietals, Cabernet is considered to have the most complex flavor, which can change greatly with age. In fact, aging is recommended—it can have a biting tannic flavor if not aged long enough. When you come to the Cabernet, old chum, you might be able to pick out flavors of currants, figs, herbs and spices, mint, leather, woods of eucalyptus and cedar, and the various berries—black-, blue-, and cran-.

Serve with: A wide range of meat and game dishes from burgers to rabbit.

Pinot Noir *(PEE-no nwahr)*: This is a wine that's described in sexual terms more than any other. Silky, supple, earthy, sweet, sexy, fleshy, firm, full-bodied, lively, exuberant, unbridled, willing, with flavors "passionately entwined...."

It's enough to give any other wine Pinots Envy.

The flavors described within include plum, truffle (the fungus, not the candy), black cherries, baked cherries, cigar, chocolate, dry leaves, damp moss, earth, wet hay, boiled beets, and prunes. Dark-colored Pinot Noirs age well; lighter colored ones have a less intense flavor and should be drunk "young."

Serve with: A wide range of meat and game dishes.

Gamay Beaujolais *(ga-may bo-zho-LAY)*: Unlike most red wines, this is one that is best served "young," not aged. Gamay grapes are also often used to produce California rosé. Technically, "Beaujolais" is a wine region in France next to

Burgundy, so some California winemakers drop that part of the name. The flavor is light and fruity. Some experts suggest serving it at a little colder temperature than most reds (sixty degrees Fahrenheit), but not as cold as whites.

Serve with: Gamay isn't a bad "compromise" wine if everyone at the table has ordered something different and you're too cheap to order two or three different wines. Works with mild game dishes, poultry, pork, ham, lamb, and fish.

Zinfandel *(ZIN-fen-del):* Zinfandel aficionados in the United States have become increasingly cult-like in their patriotic pride over this wine. Sure, those classic European wines have their appreciators, but Zin fans see themselves as championing a good, democratic, true-blue *All-American* wine. Well, almost. Like most 100 percent Americans, Zin apparently came from somewhere else before making its name here. Zinfandel was grown as a table grape in New England in the 1830s. In 1848, cuttings were transported to California where Zin's wine potential was quickly discovered. For more than a century the origins of Zinfandel were a mystery until an Italian grape, *Primitivo*, was found to be closely related, genetically.

Zinfandel is a red wine; true Zinophiles believe that the very popular so-called "White Zinfandel" (see page 28) is an abomination in the eyes of God and Man. True Zinfandel is so purple that it looks like it was artificially colored by the Kool-Aid company; Zin fans wear temporarily purpled teeth, tongue, and lips as a badge of honor. The flavor is characterized as "rustic and juicy," containing elements of an old-fashioned State Fair kitchen competition: blackberry jam, cherry pie, strawberry jellies, and baking spices.

Serve with: Red meat, veal, rabbit, game, seasoned poultry, and tomato sauce dishes.

Merlot *(mehr-LOW):* Considered to be Cabernet Sauvignon's slightly less clever brother, the two are often confused in blind taste tests, even by experts. It is a kinder, gentler wine, often blended into Cabernet to get rid of some of the tannin "edge." Professionals say it has a "fuzzier, furry" feel in the mouth compared to Cabernet's "more angular" sharpness. Merlot's flavors are compared with baked cherries, plums, black currents, chocolate, and sometimes leather.

Serve with: Seasoned poultry, red meats, wild game, pork, ham, and tomato sauce dishes.

Syrah / Petite Sirah *(sih-RAH) / pe-TEET sih-RAH):* Ha! Watch out for the trap. Smug wine experts will make fun of you if you confuse these two. They like to point out that Syrah (also known as Shirez) comes from the Hermitage in France's Rhône Valley, one of the world's oldest vineyards, going back 2,000 years. Petite Sirah? Nobody quite knows where it came from, but it somehow ended up in California.

If you're assaulted by a wine snob, challenge them to tell the difference in a blind wine tasting. Most can't—the wines are fairly indistinguishable from one another. Both are slightly bitter from high tannin and, despite the feminine sounding name, have flavors that are reminiscent of Daniel Boone: smoke, leather, old spice, smoke, tar, and pepper.

Serve with: Spicier dishes, red meats, game.

Grenache *(gre-NAWSH):* Another light-bodied wine most often used for blending, Grenache has begun showing up with more frequency as a varietal. It's often described as "floral" and "smoky."

Serve with: Spicy fish and Mexican food, where its lightness can act as a contrasting "chaser" to the spiciness.

Barbera *(bar-BEAR-a):* Barbera grapes are planted all over the world because the vine tolerates hot weather well. Dismissed by some as a "spaghetti wine" because it's a good, strong, basic wine without pretensions, Barbera ends up in a lot of boxes and jugs with screw-on tops. Some winemakers ferment it with the skins of other grapes like Petite Sirah or Zinfandel and then blend it with other wines to give it more subtle flavors than it normally comes with naturally. Fruity, tart, and high in acid, Barbera is not usually rhapsodized about in high-flown wine talk.

Serve with: Seasoned red meats, stews, wild game, and anything made with tomato sauce.

Carignan *(car-een-YAN):* Like Barbera, *"Vin ordinaire"* is what you're supposed to say dismissively about a bottle of Carignan. It's the basic jug wine of France and Spain, and is grown in California mostly as a "blending grape" (the wine equivalent of "cereal filler") or as generic "California Red." Still, you might occasionally run across it as a varietal. And even if you don't, if you are serving cheap jug wine to friends (from a carafe, of course), being able to announce that you're serving "Carignan" sounds a lot classier than calling it "generic red."

Serve with: Red meats, tomato sauce dishes, stews.

Chianti *(key-AN-tee):* Chianti has had to travel a long road toward gaining a decent reputation. Chianti used to cost almost nothing, and it came in straw-covered bottles. (The bottles were a holdover from the 1600s, when Italians wrapped glass flasks with straw or wicker to prevent breakage in shipping.) Many people bought it as much for the bottle as the wine, using the empties as vases and candleholders. All those wax-covered Chianti bottles on Beatnik-era tables led to the perception that Chianti was not to be taken seriously. Now, however, Chianti comes in a variety of qualities and styles. Although considered a red wine, it is actually a blend of red Sangiovese grapes and various white ones like Trebbiano and Malvasia.

Serve with: Italian pastas with meat sauces, chicken, pigeons (if you live near an urban park and are quick with your hands), and various grilled meats.

Other Reds: Claret is a British term denoting any red wine. **Charbono** is *not* the lady who used to be married to Sonny, but rather a hearty Italian wine which is sometimes bottled in California as well. Ditto **Nebbiolo**. There are a number of minor varietals like **Cabernet Franc, Cinsault, Mourvedre,** and **Tempranillo** that are used in mixes, concoctions, and blends. In the *vino del cheapo* class, we have generic Californian wines in boxes and jugs with misleading generic names like **burgundy** and **Chianti.**

THOSE PINK WINES

> "'I rather like bad wine,' said Mr. Mountchesney; 'one gets so bored with good wine.'"
> —Benjamin Disraeli (1804–1881), *Sybil*

There's only one word to remember if you're thinking of serving a pink wine to a serious wine drinking crowd: *Don't.*

Pink wines, whether called "rosé," "blush," or "White Zinfandel," are considered at best a beginner's wine without character, at worst a cynical marketing strategy and an affront against all that is right and good.

Making pink wines is fairly easy. Normally a red wine is

fermented with the grape skins, which give the deep color and some of the subtleties of flavor. If a winemaker presses the fermenting juice out of its skins early, the wine doesn't absorb all of the color (or flavor).

Some rosé Zinfandels and Cabernets aren't bad as a libation on a summer afternoon, but most serious wine drinkers believe that the thin fruitiness lacks something. Ironically, more White Zinfandel is now sold each year than the real stuff, leading to the comment overheard in a wine store: "You mean they make a *red* Zinfandel, too?"

THOSE CRAZY EUROPEANS

Leave it to the Europeans to make things complicated and inefficient. Like the metric system and multi-party governments, the Europeans have stubbornly maintained their own method of labeling wines. Instead of identifying the varietal on the bottles, they identify the *geographic area* where the wine was grown. It seems crazy. If American winemakers did the same thing, all the different wines, red and white, from Napa Valley would be called merely "Napa."

However, there is one saving virtue practiced by those wily foreigners: They usually grow only one (or two, or a handful of ...) varietal of grape in each of their famously identified regions. So, with a good memory, or the decoder below, you will know that any French red wine labeled "Burgundy" is not only from the province of that same name, but also a Pinot Noir. Or if it's labeled "Chianti," it's a blend of mostly Sangiovese grapes and some whites. On the other hand, if it says "Bordeaux" it could be a whole lot of things: Cabernet Sauvignon, Merlot, Cabernet Franc, and/or other minor varietals. Another reason, I guess, to "Buy American."

Place	Varietal
Beaujolais	Gamay
Bordeaux (red)	Cabernet Sauvignon, Merlot, Cabernet Franc, and/or other minor varietals
Bordeaux (white)	Sauvignon Blanc and/or Sèmillon
Burgundy (red)	Pinot Noir
Burgundy (white)	Chardonnay
Chablis	Chardonnay
Chianti	Sangiovese, blended with minor varietals
Piedmont	Nebbiolo, Barbera, and/or Dolcetto
Pouilly Fumé	Sauvignon Blanc
Northern Rhone (red)	Syrah
Southern Rhone, or Côtes du Rhone (red)	Syrah, Grenache, Cinsault, Mourvedre, and/or Carignan
Northern or Southern Rhone (white)	Viognier, Marsanne, Rousanne, other minor varietals
Rioja (red)	Tempranillo blended with Garnacha (Grenache, in Spanish)
Sancerre	Sauvignon Blanc

Blood & Wine

You think that the gentility of wine has a civilizing effect on the people who make it? Think again, my friend. Take a look at some of the family secrets, squabbles, suicides, murders, and feuds behind California's best-known wineries.

Gallo Winery

Giuseppe ("Joe") Gallo was a moody, uncommunicative, violent man who had been a saloonkeeper until Prohibition put him out of business. At that time he shifted to growing wine grapes, which he sold all over the country, ostensibly for home winemakers who were allowed to legally ferment 200 gallons a year. (In reality, many were bootleggers making a lot more than that.) His oldest sons, Ernest and Julio, were drafted into working long, thankless hours on the family farm. Their brother, Joseph Jr., was a decade younger. By the time he was old enough to help, the family's fortunes had improved and he was able to enjoy the childhood that his older brothers never had. Like his Biblical namesake, Joseph was heartily resented by his brothers, and paid for his favored position later.

Joe Sr.'s brother Mike got out of jail in 1918 and offered him a more lucrative job than growing grapes on swampy soil in Antioch, California, for illegal winemakers. Mike had been serving five years in San Quentin for running a "bunko ring" and for bribing fifteen San Francisco bunko squad cops. He saw that the fastest way to make a quick buck during Prohibition was to sell alcoholic drinks, and opened the San Pablo Bottling Shop in Oakland as a cover for his distribution system. Joe was hired to supervise the production of brandy and wine. In 1922, Joe was arrested for running an illegal brandy still. Mike made a few calls to friends in high places and the charges were mysteriously dropped.

By 1925, Joe had accumulated enough money to move to Modesto and build an $8,000 home on the edge of seventy acres of prime vineyards he paid for with cash. He began shipping grapes again on a much larger scale. He also apparently continued winemaking. One night in total, secretive darkness, Joe Jr. woke up to find his father digging a wide, deep hole with his tractor for a 32,000 gallon underground tank.

By winter of 1929, Joe was doing well enough to buy 160 more acres across the street from his house, this time paying $25,000 in cash. Julio and Ernest, full of late-teen contempt of their father, graduated from high school and worked for him, battling him periodically to raise their thirty-dollar-a-month pay and hand over shares of the business. In 1933, anticipating the end of Prohibition, Ernest applied to the government to open a bonded wine storeroom in San Francisco, but his application was turned down because he didn't own a winery—it was all in his father's name.

That changed suddenly the next day. The parents were found mysteriously dead of gunshot wounds on the family farm. After a hasty inquest, in which Ernest testified that maybe they'd had financial reverses or something, their deaths were ruled a murder-suicide.

The three brothers were supposed to inherit equal thirds

of the business, but Ernest immediately began maneuvering, according to author Ellen Hawkes in *Blood and Wine*. "While his two brothers mourned ... Ernest received permission from the probate court to continue his father's business." He applied for a winery permit twelve days after his parents' death in the name of himself and Julio, effectively cutting their younger brother out of his one-third inheritance. He essentially became their employee; he was chastised and fired for "an unwillingness to work hard" after he took a week's vacation.

Years later the two brothers would successfully sue him for using his own last name on a line of cheese; he in turn sued them unsuccessfully for a percentage of the Gallo winery. (The judge, who had been a partner in the Fresno law firm that represented Ernest and Julio, ruled that Joseph wasn't actually able to prove that his brothers had overtly defrauded him out of his inheritance.)

Neither brother knew much about making wine; they eventually got started by taking a pamphlet out of the Modesto Public Library. Julio took over the wine-manufacturing part of the business and Ernest, the marketing. "Ernest is the embodiment of the Hobbesian view of the world," one ex-employee was quoted as saying: "Nasty, brutish, and short." Ernest had a favorite saying: "Remember, people aren't led—they're driven!"

The Gallo brothers built a successful company using hard-nosed competitive tactics. Its sales force was notorious for sabotaging the competition with tricks like counterscrewing the bottle caps tightly so that they couldn't be taken off, or puncturing the caps with icepicks so the wine would go bad, or spraying a thin layer of oil on the bottles so they would quickly acquire a layer of dust, making them look like they had been there forever without selling. They deliberately littered ghetto neighborhoods with empty Thunderbird bottles to "advertise" the brand.

Building an empire on a foundation of cheap, flavored, alcohol-fortified wines deliberately designed to appeal to heavy drinkers in African-American neighborhoods, the Gallo company moved up the class chain to $60 Cabernets. Their winery factories in Modesto and Livingston are the size of oil refineries, pumping out 40% of all wine made in California, one-quarter of all wine sold in the United States—about seventy million cases a year.

Charles Krug Winery
Robert Mondavi Winery

In 1861, a young immigrant from Prussia named Charles Krug founded one of Napa Valley's first wineries. Over the following decades, the Charles Krug Winery served as a training ground for a new generation of pioneer winemakers, as a number of Krug's ungrateful employees, including Carl Wente, Jacob Schram, and the Beringer Brothers, left and started their own wineries.

Krug's death and Prohibition put the winery on hiatus; the whole operation, lock, stock, barrel, and illustrious name, was put up for sale. In 1943, an Italian immigrant named Cesare Mondavi bought it for $75,000 and, with the help of his two sons, Peter and Robert, rebuilt the Krug winery. To upgrade the wines, they replaced industrial-grade grape vines with higher-grade varietals like Riesling, Pinot Noir, and Cabernet Sauvignon.

In 1959, Cesare died. The two brothers split into warring camps. In 1965, their mom, Rosa, took Peter's side in the struggle, being quoted as saying, "I have two sons. One has short legs and he is a saint. One has longer legs and he is a devil."

Robert, the long-legged one, left the family winery and started his own down the road. The Robert Mondavi Winery ended up surpassing the family winery in both stature and sales. Robert distinguished himself in the Napa Valley as an industry spokesman by introducing classic European methods of winemaking, by introducing Chenin Blanc to the American wine drinker, and by "inventing" Fumé Blanc. He founded the American Institute of Wine and Food with Julia Child in 1981, and teamed up with French winemaker Phillippe de Rothschild to issue Opus One premium wines in 1984.

Sebastiani Winery
Viansa Winery

The Sebastiani Winery was founded during Prohibition by Samuele Sebastiani and the Gallo Brothers' crooked Uncle Mike (see above). At some point Mike was indicted for bootlegging, so he quickly sold his share of the winery to Samuele.

Samuele's son August eventually took over the family business and was able to make a big success of it, creating the second largest family winery in the United States, exceeded only by Gallo. Finally, though, it was clear that his reign was coming to an end.

"Sam will be the one to run the winery," August Sabastian predicted of his sons months before he died in 1980, "and Don will be the politician."

August's prediction turned out to be true for many years: Sam, Don's elder by twelve years, managed the winery, while little brother Don became a rabidly archconservative politician who used his money and connections to get elected to the California state assembly.

That was the beginning of the problem. Don was so retrograde that his nickname in the assembly was "Caveman Don." He became notorious for outspoken opposition to such things as equal pay for women and recognition for Martin Luther King, Jr. In 1986, for example, he voted against a tribute to the first female astronaut Sally Ride, explaining with gross insensitivity, "I don't mind lady astronauts, as long as they only have a one-way ticket."

Another time, he argued against funding for AIDS research. "There is a tooth fairy, Santa Claus wears green tennis shoes, the moon is made of gorgonzola cheese, and I can tell you with equal assurance that ... AIDS is not a gay disease," Sebastiani said sarcastically, adding, "All three words, AIDS, gay, and disease, are synonymous with one another."

Faced with a consumer boycott against Sebastiani wine because of Caveman Don, Sam issued an ultimatum: Either retire from politics, or cut ties with the winery. He sent Don a telegram: "I will do everything I can to see you defeated. I cannot tolerate your active abuse of my efforts and our good name."

Don, loving the public notoriety, reluctantly resigned his position at the winery (although he continued to reap the profits) thereby narrowly averting a boycott.

But it was just the beginning of the war inside the family. Don, resentful about being asked to make a choice, began complaining to his mother, Sylvia, who owned a controlling share of stocks. She was silent at first, but in 1985, Sylvia came to a high-level sales meeting to announce that Don was thinking of running for Lieutenant Governor and she wanted assurances that nobody at the winery, particularly Sam, would say anything critical about his campaign. She added, "If you treat Don like you did before, I'm going to do something drastic."

"I am a 45-year-old man," Sam snapped back "I don't want to be treated like a child." After Sylvia departed, a flabbergasted Sam told the executives, "I've just had my day ruined," and adjourned the meeting. Sam had already worried and angered his family by spending $6 million to modernize the company plant. He did this in order to branch into quality wines to augment the slipping market in the cheap jug wines the company had always made.

Don ended up running for State Controller. He lost, and was out of a job ... but not for long. In 1986, Sylvia fired Sam, and put Don in charge of the winery.

"Don could do no wrong in Sylvia's eyes," a former winery official was quoted as saying. "When he made that outrageous comment about female astronauts, her attitude was, 'That's just Don—he just says those things sometimes.'"

Sam went off and started the Sam J. Sebastiani Winery. After it became clear that neither winery was being helped by the confusion between the two names, Sam changed the name to Viansa Winery, a coinage from "Vicki (his wife) and Sam," and began producing limited quantities of premium wines.

Wine by the Numbers

- Republicans are more likely to drink wine than Democrats. That may be more a function of income level than politics, however, since 66% of families with incomes over $50,000 drink wine, as opposed to only 29% of those with incomes below $15,000.

- One ton of grapes will make about 160 gallons of wine. A ton of wine grapes normally sells for $200 to $2000. A liter bottle of wine contains between 25¢ and $2.25 worth of grapes. In many cases, the bottle, cork, and label cost more to produce than the wine inside.

- E & J Gallo Winery produces 25% of all American wine.

- California produces 90% of all American wine. New York produces 8%. All other states combined are responsible for the remaining 2%.

- The average French person drinks ten times as much wine as the average American.

- Only one continent does not produce wine: Antarctica.

- Napa and Sonoma counties combined produce only 9% of all California wines.

Champagne

Most sparkling wine drunk in America is not really Champagne. By definition, true Champagne comes from the Champagne district of France, and they can be Pinot Noir or Pinot Meunier (red), Chardonnay (white), or a combination.

Champagne is not a varietal of wine, but a process of fermentation. Most wines only go through one fermentation, but sparkling wine goes through two. The classic *mèthode champenoise* requires seventeen separate steps.

After harvesting and pressing the grapes, there's a first fermentation in big vats that takes two to three weeks. After that, the winemaker puts the wine in its bottle and adds a sugar-yeast syrup to it before "corking" it with a temporary crown cap like those used on soda pop bottles. Carbon dioxide, allowed to dissipate into the air during the first fermentation, gets trapped in the bottle in the second and, because of mounting atmospheric pressure, is unable to escape from the liquid. The gas stays imprisoned in the wine, waiting for a chance when the pressure's off to make its escape.

It waits a long time. Sparkling wine ages for six months to two years. Only one problem: Over time, the yeast cells die and sink to the bottom of the bottle, making an ugly sediment. How do you get it out without losing all the carbonation?

Ironically, the answer to this riddle is a technique called

"riddling." The bottles are placed neck down in a rack and occasionally turned and jolted over six to eight weeks so all the yeast cells settle against the cork. When it's time to disgorge the sediment, the bottle is placed—its neck still pointing down—in a supercold icy brine. The sediment freezes in the neck, forming an icy plug. The winemaker pops off the bottle cap, and pressure inside shoots the frozen plug out of the bottle.

Since there's now some wine missing from the bottle, the wine maker can determine how sweet to make the Champagne by topping it off with a *dosage* (do-SAHZH)—a blend of sugar syrup, white wine, and sometimes brandy. A little sugar makes a *brut,* more sugar makes a *sec,* a *demi-sec,* and a *doux.* (So now you know why Champagne makers look so happy—they're douxing secs all day, the bruts!)

The History of Champagne

Dom Pèrignon was a Benedictine monk in Hautvillers, near Reims in France. To his annoyance, he accidentally invented Champagne in the 1660s while trying to improve the abbey's white wine. He had been making a batch late in the season and thought that the fermentation had stopped, so he bottled it. However, some yeast remained alive and became active again the next spring when the weather warmed up, making a second fermentation inside the bottle. When he opened a bottle, he was disgusted to find that it had gone "bad" but drank some anyway. His reaction? According to legend, he blurted out, "I am drinking stars!" Still, he considered the bubbles were an unwelcome "impurity" ... until people tried the wine and popular demand for bubbly wine forced him to try to repeat the accident. With some experimentation, he came up with the basic process still used today.

Champagne was a nightmare for glassblowers. With all that pressure building up inside, a good proportion of the bottles exploded in wine cellars. Winemakers began the practice of closely inspecting every bottle upon arrival. The ones that were clearly irregular were set aside for uncarbonated red wine. The others were tested by smartly banging them together. Any that broke were charged to the glassblower; the ones that survived were deemed strong enough. Still, this was a less than foolproof method.

The exploding bottle crisis hit its peak with the vintage of 1828. Weather conditions resulted in extra sugar in the grapes that year, supercharging the fermentation process. It was a booming, bang-up year for Champagne makers as eighty percent of the vintage burst its bottles. How explosive can a Champagne bottle be, you ask? Ever have a blowout on a ten-speed bicycle? The pressure inside a Champagne bottle is normally ninety pounds per square inch, about the same as a high-pressure bike tire and three times that of an auto tire—and in 1828, the pressure was even higher than that. With shards of jagged, wine-soaked glass flying in all directions, spending time in a wine cellar became more dangerous than going to war.

As a result of the 1828 fiasco, a French chemist invented the *sucre-oenometre*, an instrument that measures sugar content in grapes. With its use, the Champagne bottle breakage rate went way down. But "way down" is a relative thing: Fifteen to twenty percent of all Champagne bottles continued to explode in storage. Wine stewards adapted their own strategies. They began storing Champagne in isolated nooks and routinely wearing wire masks when in the cellar.

Serving Champagne

In the early days of Champagne, when it was only available as a *très* sweet dessert wine, much of the appeal was to untie the string that held the cork on and shower your companions with the sticky, bubbly liquid. This was especially popular, possibly for its symbolic implications, among older men dining with pretty young women. It was fun, but it ruined the bubbliness of the Champagne for drinking.

Unfortunately, this wham-bam, thank-you-ma'am approach to sparkling wine is still common. Popping the cork across the room in one premature ejaculation not only squanders all that hard-won carbon dioxide, but it is dangerous to onlookers and innocent bystanders.

Here's a better way:

1. Sparking wine should be served cold. But not too cold. Put it in the warmest part of your refrigerator (the vegetable bin's good). If you start a party and find you forgot to chill it, however, DON'T put it in the freezer unless you set a timer, and even that can be dangerous, because in as little as fifteen minutes, a bottle of Champagne can freeze enough to explode, christening your stash of Fudgesicles, Eggos, frozen lima beans, and TV dinners. Instead, dig out that champagne bucket you got for a wedding present and never used (or in a pinch, rinse the Mr. Clean residue out of a plastic cleaning bucket). Fill it with ice and water and wait twenty minutes.

2. Remove the foil from the cork. Place one hand on top of the cork for safety, and leave it there until the cork is safely out of the bottle.

3. With another hand, remove the wire. Some corks try to pop immediately, so hold on. Wrap a towel or large napkin around the bottle.

Champagne

4. Slowly turn the cork in one direction and the bottle in the other, easing the cork out slowly and without pop or circumstance. If the wine starts cascading out, soak it up with your towel or napkin. Unless you're alone and absolutely sure nobody's watching, putting your mouth over the opening to catch the overflow is considered *very* bad form.

5. Helpful hint for young lovers: No matter how hopelessly romantic it sounds, drinking Champagne out of your beloved's shoe is a gesture that invariably turns out much better in fantasy than reality.

Rhapsody in Red, White, and Rosé

Drinking wine can be an excuse to look eloquent, cultured, and literate. You could actually go to the trouble of being well-read ... or just memorize a few of these poetic quotations to recite. They are best quoted loudly, after a glass or two, as if you were making a toast.

"Why look you now; 'tis when men drink they thrive,
Grow wealthy, speed their business, win their suits,
Make themselves happy, benefit their friends."
—Aristophanes (448–380 B.C.)

"And much as Wine has play'd the Infidel,
And robb'd me of my Robe of Honour—Well,
I often wonder what the Vintners buy
One half so precious as the Goods they sell."
—Edward Fitzgerald (1809–1883),
The Rubaiyat of Omar Khayyám

"They are not long, the days of wine and roses:
Out of a misty dream
Our path emerges for a while, then closes
Within a dream."
—Earnest Dowson (1867–1900), *Vitae Summa Brevis*

"Lo! the poor toper whose untutor'd sense,
  Sees bliss in ale, and can with wine dispense;
  Whose head proud fancy never taught to steer,
  Beyond the muddy ecstasies of beer."
                          —George Crabbe (1754–1832),
                          Inebriety, Imitation of Pope

"And Noah he often said to his wife when he sat down to dine,
  'I don't care where the water goes if it doesn't get into the wine.'"
                —G. K. Chesterton (1874–1936), *Wine and Water*

"All love at first, like generous wine,
  Ferments and frets until 'tis fine;
  But when 'tis settled on the lee,
  And from th' impurer matter free,
  Becomes the richer still the older,
  And proves the pleasanter the colder."
  —Samuel Butler (1612–1680), *Miscellaneous Thoughts*

"If all be true that I do think,
  There are five reasons we should drink;
  Good wine—a friend—or being dry—
  Or lest we should be by and by—
  Or any other reason why."
          —Dean Aldrich (1647–1710), *Reasons for Drinking*

"But that which most doth take my Muse and me,
  Is a pure cup of rich Canary wine,
  Which is the Mermaid's now, but shall be mine."
                          —Ben Jonson, (1572–1637),
                          Epigrams: Inviting a Friend to Supper

"Souls of poets dead and gone,
What Elysium have ye known,
Happy field or mossy cavern,
Choicer than the Mermaid Tavern?
Have ye tippled drink more fine
Than mine host's Canary wine?"

—John Keats (1795–1821),
Lines on the Mermaid Tavern

"O, for a draught of vintage! that hath been
Cool'd a long age in the deep-delved earth,
Tasting of Flora and the country green,
Dance, and Provencal song, and sunburnt mirth!
O for a beaker full of the warm South,
Full of the true, the blushful Hippocrene,
With beaded bubbles winking at the brim,
And purple-stained mouth;
That I might drink, and leave the world unseen,
And with thee fade away into the forest dim."

—John Keats (1795–1821),
Ode to a Nightingale

What Do You Do
When Handed the Cork?

Quiz time: You're in a restaurant. You've circumvented the pitfalls of the wine list (see page 18), and managed to order something without making a fool of yourself. Just when you've relaxed, thinking that your wine ordeal is over for the day, the waiter pulls the cork from the bottle and hands it to you. Conversation stops, and all eyes turn to you expectantly. What do you do now?

a. Sniff the cork

b. Lick it

c. Bite lustily into it

d. Nibble around the edges of it, leaving enough for your friends

e. Toss it over your left shoulder for luck

f. Slip it into your pocket or purse for the next time you go to the ol' fishin' hole

g. Pass it around the table

h. Fondle it

i. See if there's something to read on it

j. Hand it back

k. Create a diversion and lose it in the confusion

The correct answer is ... h. and i.

Fondle it, you ask, in a public place? Well, not exactly fondle it. That can be done later in the privacy of your own home. Feel it. Why? To see if it's wet. Why do you care if it's wet? Because a dry cork means that the bottle was not properly stored on its side. If dry, can you send the wine back? Well, no, but you can be snotty to the wine steward about it. "Sir," you may say reproachfully, "this bottle has not been properly stored," waving away his apologies and excuses.

Next you read the cork. You are not looking for messages like "Help, I'm being held prisoner in the wine cellar" or even "This is the poisoned one," although the smart wine drinker will take heed if such a message is found. No, you are making sure the winery information branded on the cork matches what is on the label. The little ceremony is a throwback to a century ago, when wine fraud was common. It is meant to assure you that the restaurant hasn't tried to rip you off by changing labels on the bottle. Read the cork, compare and contrast with the label, and lay the cork casually on the table. Later, you can nibble it, or put it in your pocket for the next time you go fishin', but for now, you must take part in the second part of the ceremony.

The waiter pours a splash of wine into your glass and waits expectantly. It's his little trap, just when you think you're out of the woods. DON'T DRINK IT. Instead, swirl the wine around in your glass and take one long, dramatic sniff. Hold your breath for a second in order to build suspense. Unless it smells like vinegar, you exhale, look the server in the eye, and nod once, significantly.

But what if you get that vinegary smell that evokes memories of salad, Easter egg dye, and douche? Luckily, being served wine that has turned into vinegar is a pretty rare occurrence, but if that happens, discretely tell your server, "I believe this wine has passed its peak" or " ... turned," or (if you prefer euphemism) " ... gone to meet its maker." The server will whisk it away and bring another bottle, beginning the whole process one more time.

Put a Cork in It

Good wines have corks. Bad wines have screw-on caps. Or at least that's what we've been led to believe. But after years of promoting that idea, winemakers are struggling to reverse it.

Corks began as a solution to the problem of how to plug bottles and keep the wine uncontaminated and unspilled. The Romans first used corks for this purpose, but the practice fell out of favor for some reason and was forgotten for about fourteen centuries. During the Medieval Era, they often used a twist of cloth to seal bottles, a solution that was to be revived for molotov cocktails in our time. They also tried stoppers made of leather and even sealing wax. (This latter solution likely gave critics a reason to wax eloquent on why wine was on the wane.)

Finally, corks as wine stoppers were rediscovered in the early sixteenth century, soon enough for Shakespeare to write in *As You Like It,* "I pray thee take thy cork out of thy mouth, that I may drink thy tidings." Still, ground glass stoppers continued to be preferred by many winemakers because they found, as one complained, that "much liquor [is] being absolutely spoiled by the defect of the cork." Cork-induced spoilage is still a big headache, with an estimated eight percent of all bottled wine being damaged to some degree by moldy corks which add a bouquet and flavor reminiscent of "wet cardboard."

Strangely, corkscrews didn't appear until several decades later. Before then, the cork was pushed only halfway into the bottle to make it possible to get it out again. The first mention of a "bottlescrew," described as a "steel worm used for the drawing out of corks" was recorded in 1681, and they weren't actually called "corkscrews" until 1720.

Why were corks considered so ideal for sealing wine? Well, for one thing they're very elastic because they're filled with more than 300 million tiny air-filled cells. They spring back to their original shape, even after withstanding 14,000 pounds of pressure per cubic inch. A cork can be compressed enough to get it into a bottle, yet it will immediately spring back to fill any gaps around the edge. Also, they're fairly durable, keeping their structural integrity for up to fifty years before going brittle and crumbly.

About seventy-five percent of the United State's wine corks come from Portugal—over 360 million a year. They're made from the four-inch thick, fire-resistant bark of the cork oak, a slow-growing evergreen that grows in the western Mediterranean regions. Every nine or ten years, each tree is almost completely stripped of its bark, leaving only enough to ensure that the tree will survive. A tree can be stripped twelve to fifteen times during its natural life span.

The sheets of cork are stacked for three months to dry. They're then boiled in giant vats filled with fungicides, dried again, and then cut into bottle-sized, tapered cylinders that cost wine bottlers about twenty to forty cents each.

That's a lot, sometimes more than the wine itself costs to make. It drives vintners crazy sometimes, because they know corks are only one of the ways of sealing bottles, and not even the best way. Screw tops, for example, are at least as good and only cost a nickel each. One vague but prevailing myth is that the cork is somehow better because it lets the wine "breathe." Actually, wines don't need to "breathe"— in fact, one of the best ways to end up with vinegar instead of wine is to have a cork that lets air leak in. Yet consumers have learned to associate a cork with good wine and have so far resisted change in any but the cheapest wines.

Wine in the Bible

Odds are, sometime or another, you'll run across ultra-conservative Christians who believe their God forbids the use of wine. In fact, the Bible mentions wine no less than 191 times, giving permission for believers to use wine as long as they don't misuse it. Regardless, a couple of the early passages in the Bible are a bit bizarre. For example, in Genesis 9:20–28, Noah plants a vineyard, makes wine, gets drunk and lies "uncovered" in his tent. His son, Ham, accidentally sees his nakedness. Noah, hungover and outraged, curses Ham and his descendants, making them the slaves of his brothers.

And then in Genesis 19:30–38, Lot's virgin daughters, left motherless and without their fiancés by the destruction of Sodom and Gomorrah, get their father drunk on wine each night and seduce him until both get pregnant. They eventually bear him sons and grandsons in one fell swoop. God—who earlier had turned Lot's wife into salt for a single backward glance at the destruction of her hometown—exacted no retribution, leading to the conclusion that drunkenness and incest are less of a sin than curiosity.

Notable Bible Quotations

"Therefore God give thee of the dew of heaven, and the fatness of the earth, and plenty of corn and wine."—Genesis 27:28

"Do not drink wine nor strong drink, thou, nor thy sons with thee, when ye go into the tabernacle of the congregation, lest ye die: it shall be a statute for ever throughout your generations."—Leviticus 10:9

"Thou hast showed thy people hard things: thou hast made us to drink the wine of astonishment."—Psalms 60:3

"And wine maketh glad the heart of man."—Psalms 104:15

"Wine is a mocker, strong drink is raging: and whosoever is deceived thereby is not wise."—Proverbs 20:1

"He that loveth pleasure shall be a poor man: he that loveth wine and oil shall not be rich."—Proverbs 21:17

"Look not thou upon the wine when it is red, when it giveth his colour in the cup, when it moveth itself aright. . . . Thy eyes will see strange things, and thy mind utter perverse things."—Proverbs 23:31

"Give strong drink unto him that is ready to perish, and wine unto those that be of heavy hearts."—Proverbs 31:6

"Go thy way, eat thy bread with joy, and drink thy wine with a merry heart; for God now accepteth thy works."—Ecclesiastes 9:7

"A feast is made for laughter, and wine maketh merry: but money answereth all things."—Ecclesiastes 10:19

"Drink no longer water, but use a little wine for thy stomach's sake and thine often infirmities."—Timothy 5:23

Serving Wine

Serving wine? What's the big deal? You just pour from the bottle into more or less clean glasses, right?

True, that'll work ... but so will putting the bottle into a paper bag and passing it around the table for each of your guests to take a swig. The difference between merely serving wine and doing it right requires a bit more than a bottle and glasses—even if they all match, and even if they've all got the same picture of Charlie Brown and Snoopy on their sides.

Temperature

In the fourth century, B.C., Hippocrates, the father of medicine, had some firm ideas about the proper temperature for serving wine. He believed that drinking warm wine would eventually lead to "imbecility," while imbibing cold wine led to "convulsions, rigid spasms, mortifications, and chilling horrors, terminating in a fever."

Luckily, wine experts nowadays are slightly less alarmist about getting the serving temperature right. Still, there is some consensus: The temperature of the wine should be cool for whites and warmer for reds. Refrigerator cold is too cold for either. Whites are meant to be served at a temperature of about fifty to fifty-five degrees, so refrigerate it and then take it out a while before drinking, or store it at room temperature and chill it a little before serving.

In the old days, when houses and castles were somewhat cooler and more drafty than today, they used to say to serve red wine "at room temperature." But normal room temperature now is too warm. What's called "cellar" temperature is best, about sixty to sixty-five degrees, the temperature of a wine exposed to room temperature for a few minutes after coming out of a good wine cellar.

Decanting and "Breathing": Death to the Zinfandel!

Is it good for wines to be poured from a container besides the original bottle they came in? Do red wines need to be allowed to "breathe" before serving?

You might as well ask how many angels can dance on the cork of a Pinot Noir. The cases for and against decanting and "breathing" are so rooted in opposing articles of faith that it seems that both camps are ready to take up torches and begin shouting, "Decant your heresy! Death to the Zinfandel!"

The good news is that, in contrast to the issue of wine glasses, decanting requires no particular shape container size. In fact, it probably isn't even necessary. There are really only a few reasons to take the wine out of its original bottle and put it in another. They are:

1. **Sediment.** If you've got an old bottle of wine and there is a bunch of unidentifiable but murky stuff at the bottom, be careful not to disturb it when you open the bottle. Instead, position a light—a candle, flashlight, or low-watt bulb—so you can see through the wine and wine bottle. Start pouring it slowly into the decanter until just before you get to the murky stuff. Then stop. You can save the murky stuff and drink it yourself later—it's still good wine, just not as pretty, and a little chewier than normal.

2. **Color.** Some people decant wine for the pure visual beauty of looking at the color of the wine outside its tinted bottle.

3. **Disguise.** Still others repackage the wine so that their guests won't be distracted by looking at the prestigious label and thinking about how expensive this wine is ... or conversely, by looking at the label and thinking, "They're really going to serve this cheap stuff to us?" Richard Nixon, while still in the White House, reportedly used the decanter trick to disguise the fact that he was being served a much better wine than his guests.

4. **Odors.** The most controversial reason to decant is to let the wine "breathe" before serving it. Some wine experts still claim that red wines need to be opened and exposed to air for specified time periods ranging from thirty minutes to overnight. The idea is that some old red wines developed sulfurous off-smells that needed to be dissipated. The simple act of pouring the wine from the bottle to a decanter oxygenates it to some degree and letting it sit will continue the process. It is clear that letting wine sit open at room temperature will have some effect on its flavor. The only question, still hotly debated, is whether the flavor is improved ... or seriously degraded. Many experts seem to believe that most wines don't need aeration. If you get a glass of wine that smells like Old Faithful, they say, you can aerate efficiently by simply swirling it in your glass until the smell passes.

Wine Glasses

"Glasses are placed in a semi-circle either in front of the plate or else on the right; arrange these according to the courses to be served. First, water glass; second, white wine; third,

sherry; fourth, Rhine wine; fifth, champagne; and sixth, Bordeaux. . . . Glasses intended for dessert wines and liquors, are only put on the table with dessert."—Nineteenth-century wine expert Charles Ranhofer in *The Epicurean,* 1893

There has been a lot of foolishness about the proper shapes and sizes of wine glasses. This folly has passed from generation to generation through centuries of superstition and misguided tradition. Luckily, though, we live in enlightened times, where we can rip away the veil of old traditions and discredited assumptions and establish a new tradition, based on new, modern assumptions that have not been discredited . . . yet.

In years past, you were expected to have a different shape of glass for every kind of wine you might serve. A century ago, for example, each of the red wines would be served in various large, rounded glasses; the white wines, in smaller, less tapered ones. You served Champagne in a "coupe"—a shallow, wide-mouthed glass you still continue to see today, even though wine experts universally deplore them.

In our brave new world, however, the enlightened wisdom of our times demands just two different kinds of glasses. (Or maybe three, depending on whose enlightened wisdom you choose to believe. Or maybe four, if you count the Snoopy glasses. Wine experts regularly find themselves in glass warfare on this subject.) The two ideal wine glasses, according to the experts, are one shape for bubbly wine, and another for everything else.

Let's start with the "everything else" glasses. They should have stems that prevent your hands from warming the wine. They should also be unusually large. Most experts suggest a size between ten and sixteen ounces, a few think they should be even larger. The size of the glasses is not to encourage overindulgence in drinking, but rather to allow a lot of enclosed airspace above the wine. You should be able to pour in the usual serving of wine—three or four ounces—and still have a glass that is less than half full. There are several reasons for this, all related to the wine-tasting ritual (see page 68). One is to give you and your guests a chance to swirl the wine around in the glass without splatter-painting the entire room, which happens more often than you'd think. Another is to allow for a good collection of the wine fumes for you to sniff before drinking.

To see wine clearly, stemmed, oversized glasses, without engraving, colors, or cut patterns should be used. Finally they should be "tulip shaped"—curved inward at the top to collect the scent ("the nose") of the wine and to decrease the amount of spillage from guests who have become snockered and slovenly, especially when they begin swirling wine around. Wine glasses with a good shape have been favorably compared to a Franklin stove, those great potbellied woodburners designed by Benjamin Franklin himself: bulbous at the bottom, round in the middle, and tapered gracefully to a "chimney" at the top. (It's been suggested rather cruelly that Franklin seems to have modeled the stove after himself.)

But despite disagreement about a lot of things, experts nearly unanimously agree that Champagne and other bubbling wines should not be served in rounded "tulip" glasses. Nor should they be served in those awful plastic "Champagne glasses" popular at wedding receptions. They have been scientifically proven to be unsuited for a bubbly beverage. The wide bottom releases the bubbles too fast, turning the wine flat in minutes. Instead, a good Champagne glass is narrow rather than broad, it has a tapered bottom to give a good launching pad for the display of bubbles, and, like the standard wine glass, its top tapers inward. The favorite shapes of Champagne experts are a taller, skinnier version of the "tulip," or the "flute" which is straight and relatively untapered.

There is the third glass "controversy." Some connoisseurs believe a smallish and narrow glass, holding four to six ounces, for port or sherry is mandatory. Others believe that the third glass is an unnecessary complication—that the standard, larger tulip glass will do the trick.

The last thing to think about when buying wine glasses is that they should be sturdy, unless you're intending to throw them into the fireplace after the first toast. Wine glasses go through a lot of accidental banging and deliberate clinking. Many thin and dainty glasses break quickly and chip easily in use or while washing.

Should wine glasses be washed lovingly by hand using the best dish detergent? No. Standard dishwashing liquids contain fats and glycerin. Even if you rinse fanatically and with *very* hot water, a film may stay on the glass which some wine drinkers believe can throw the taste of a wine off slightly. Whether or not you're sensitive enough to taste that, avoiding dish soap is especially important when washing your Champagne glasses. Bubbles will fail to form in a glass with the slightest trace of detergent, greasy film, or dust.

Some wine fanatics never wash their glasses in any kind of soap, merely rinsing them in water, figuring that the wine will kill any remaining germs.

One school of thought says you should run dirty wine glasses through the dishwasher, but without the soap. Another says to use the dishwasher detergent, but not the dishwasher— they wash the glasses by hand, but use dishwasher powder to scrub the wine glasses to a bright shine, because it rinses cleanly without a trace.

The fact that both swear by their method indicates that either probably works. Which means that there's no reason why a best of both worlds approach shouldn't also work: Put your wine glasses in the dishwasher, put the soap in, and let it run. Easy!

Champagne Glasses:
Keeping Abreast of Marie Antoinette

There's a great old wine legend, so good that it's almost a shame to knock it down. The bowl of the historic but now discredited Champagne glass, wide, full, and shallow, was alleged to have been directly modeled from Marie ("let 'em eat cake") Antoinette's right breast.

The myth was apparently a garbling of history. At the request of King Louis XVI, a porcelain company made a mold from one of Marie Antoinette's firm, round breasts from which they created four porcelain bowls. One remains on display in the Queen's Dairy Temple at the Chateau de Rambouillet. But those bowls were never intended for Champagne, or any other kind of wine.

The rounded Champagne glass came out in 1840, several decades after Marie Antoinette lost her head to both Champagne and the guillotine.

Wine, Women, and Song

"Wine, Women, and Song" may sound quaint though sexist now, but a century or two ago it was the wild-eyed sensualist's equivalent of our more modern "Sex, Drugs, and Rock 'n' Roll." Not even stern religious leader Martin Luther (who, but the way, was also obsessed with bowling) could apparently resist its charms.

> *"Wer nicht liebt Wein, Weib und Gesang,*
> *Der bleibt ein Narr sein Leben lang."*
> (Who loves not woman, wine, and song
> Remains a fool his whole life long.)
> —Attributed to Martin Luther (1483–1546)

> "Let us have wine and women, mirth and laughter,
> Sermons and soda-water the day after."
> —Lord Byron (1788–1824), *Don Juan*

> "Fill ev'ry glass, for wine inspires us,
> And fires us
> With courage, love and joy.
> Women and wine should life employ.
> Is there ought else on earth desirous?"
> —John Gay (1685–1732), *Air XIX*

"Choose wine you mean shall serve you all the year,
Well-flavoured, tasting well, and coloured clear.
Five qualities there are, wine's praise advancing,
Strong, Beautiful, and Fragrant, cool, and dancing. . . .
Wine, women, baths, by art or nature warm,
Used or abused, do men much good or harm."
> —Sir John Harington, godson of Queen Elizabeth,
> who also, incidentally, is credited with inventing the
> modern flush toilet, 1586

"A Book of Verses underneath the Bough,
A Jug of Wine, a Loaf of Bread—and Thou
Beside me singing in the Wilderness—
Oh, Wilderness were Paradise enow!"
> —Edward Fitzgerald (1809–1883),
> *The Rubaiyat of Omar Khayyám*

"Oh some are fond of Spanish wine, and some are fond
of French,
And some'll swallow tay and stuff fit only for a wench.
Oh some are fond of fiddles, and a song well sung,
And some are all for music for to lilt upon the tongue;
But mouths were made for tankards, and for sucking at
the bung,
Says the old bold mate of Henry Morgan."
> —John Masefield (1878–1967),
> *Captain Stratton's Fancy*

"Give me books, fruit, French wine and fine weather and a
little music out of doors, played by somebody I do not know."
> —John Keats (1795–1821)

Wine, Women, and Song

"I may not here omit those two main plagues, and common dotages of human kind, wine and women, which have infatuated and besotted myriads of people. They go commonly together."

—Robert Burton (1577–1640),
Democritus to the Reader

Celebrity Winemakers

"I don't think you'll find a single celebrity owning a winery who doesn't truly love wine. They were into the wine thing well before they owned a winery."
—W. R. Tish, *Wine Enthusiast* magazine

Owning a vineyard or a winery is an idle dream for many, combining the pastoral fantasies of farm life, fresh air, bottles with your name on them, and lots of free drinks. But who has the required combination of money, ego, social-climber aspirations, and free time? One group that has them in spades is the underworked and overpaid workers of the entertainment industry. What many entertainers, and a few renegade business leaders, really want, it appears, is to become respectable country squires.

"It tells me these people have too much money," says one wine expert. "Owning a winery is a good way to make a small fortune out of a large fortune."

• Actor Fess Parker. ("Sometimes I think someone slipped a little peyote in my Ovaltine," said TV's Davy Crockett. "Producing wine is difficult, but there's a lot of satisfaction in it.")

• Former Chrysler Chairman Lee Iacocca. (Remember, don't drink and drive.)

Celebrity Winemakers

• Film director Francis Ford Coppola. (He owns the Niebaum-Coppola Estate, a 1,700-acre property, a supplier to Inglenook, that was one of California's earliest vineyards. Presumably, he makes a wine you can't refuse.)

• *Jeopardy*'s Alex Trebek. ("I'll take a Zinfandel for $200, Alex.")

• Folk singer comedians Smothers Brothers. (Their "Mom's Favorite White" wine neatly alludes to one of their most famous punchlines.)

• Deadpan political satirist Pat Paulsen. (Dry, very dry.)

• TV actor Wayne Rogers. (He owns Continental Vineyards, presumably with a specialty of M*A*S*Hing the grapes.)

• Members of the Walt Disney Family. (They own Silverado Vineyards, *not* some Mickey Mouse little deal.)

• Steven Seagal. (Wine with a kick.)

• Jean-Claude Van Damme. (Wine with a karate chop.)

• Gerard Depardieu (California wine with a French accent.)

• There's even a Marilyn Merlot, licensed by the estate of the late actress. (A little tart, but a great body.) What's next, a Jimmy Durante Chianti? ("Impressive nose!")

Wine Tasting

"Italians when they drink, do it in stages and small quantities at a time, examining and re-examining the wine just as physicians do with urine, and they taste it repeatedly, chewing it slowly between their teeth until they have drunk it all. Those who dwell, think, and cogitate ceaselessly about wine, speaking, writing, following and moulding themselves to it, will suffer the consequences."

—Francesc Eiximenis, fourteenth-century
Catalan author, *Lo Crestia*

Wine has been around a lot longer than wine tastings. But in prehistory, after wine was first invented by accident, wine most likely tasted pretty foul. Even if people had the words to express it, their wines would not "amuse the palate with its fruity effervescence"—it would make a strong man blanch. They drank it because it made them satisfactorily drunk, and because they hadn't figured out how to make beer yet.

The first recorded wine snobbery was in the Bible. Jesus, at a wedding, was reported in the book of John to have changed water into wine midway through a wedding party. The chief steward tasted it (presumably after swirling and sniffing it) and said, "Everyone serves the good wine first, and then the inferior wine after the guests have become drunk. But you have kept the good wine until now." He didn't, at least, say anything about the wine's "fruity effervescence."

HOW TO KEEP FROM EMBARRASSING YOURSELF AT A WINE TASTING

"Note that some wine dealers cheat.... They make bitter and sour wines appear sweet by persuading the tasters to first eat licorice or nuts or old salty cheese.... Wine tasters can protect themselves against such doings by tasting wine in the morning after they have rinsed their mouths and eaten three or four bites of bread dipped in water, for whoever tries out a wine on a quite empty or on a quite full stomach will find his mouth and his tasting spoiled."
—Arnaldus de Villanova, *Liber de Vinis*, 1311

"What's with all this swirling, twirling, sniffing, sipping, and gargling anyway?" That's the first thing a novice wonders at a wine tasting. The second thing is, "Hey, why are those idiots spitting out perfectly good wine?"

Well, the spitting part doesn't happen at all wine tastings. At amateur tastings, people swallow. Professional tasters, though, might go through fifty different wines in one session. If the tasters swallowed every time, their reviews would quickly deteriorate from "A silky suppleness with a rich, mellow fruitiness" to "I'LL FIGHT ANYBODY WHO SAYS THIS STUFF AIN'T PRETTY DAMN GOOD!"

One thing is certain: People at a wine tasting alternate between looking pretentious and doing things that are incomprehensible to a normal person like you and me. But there's a reason for it all. Here's what you should do to make it look like you know what you're doing, and go on to the next step: mastering the pretentiousness.

1. Stare intently at the wine.

"Look at the wine? Why? Who cares what it looks like?" you may ask. But there are good reasons to look, both for

aesthetic enjoyment and to see what you are going to taste. Besides, when you lift up your glass and stare at it, you look like you're thinking of making a toast, which always gets other people's attention.

First the aesthetic reasons: Wine held up to a well-lit, white background is really quite pretty. White wines range from the bubble-filled, light straw color of the Champagnes to the deep golds of the Sauternes; red wines, from the light cherry red of an Italian Valpolicella to the rich ruby red of a Rhone Valley Côte Rotie.

But there's another, more practical reason to look: You want to look for evidence of spoilage and other problems before you taste. Cloudiness, for example, tells you that the yeast is still at work and the wine isn't ready to drink. An odd tinge of brown can tell you that the wine has aged too much and is moving toward becoming a very expensive salad dressing. Anything floating or sitting in the wine is also a reason to look closer. Usually flotsam and jetsam in wine are just pieces of cork or other harmless residue, but if they turn out to be something else—for example, broken glass or something with legs and wings—you want to know that before bringing the glass to your lips.

2. Swirl the wine around in your glass and sniff.

Maybe you remember what you learned in elementary school: Your taste buds can sense only sweet, sour, salty, and bitter, and most of what you think you "taste" actually comes from your sense of smell. Well, your teacher didn't lie to you this time.

Wine experts augment their natural abilities by using an elementary science trick. They swirl the wine around in the glass by holding its stem and twisting their wrists back and forth. Swirling covers the inside of your glass with a thin sheet of wine, causing it to evaporate more quickly into the air and dramatically increasing its aroma. Good wine glasses taper slightly inward to capture that "bouquet," as wine folk call it. (Some fanatics insist that it must be swirled *clockwise*, for some reason. This, of course, is superstitious claptrap. Presumably, if you happen to live in the Southern Hemisphere, they insist it should be swirled counter-clockwise.)

Immediately after you swirl, stick your nose down *into* the glass and sniff. You may be pleasantly surprised how many more details of the wine you can smell. If you can't smell much, it might be that the wine doesn't have much of a bouquet, or it could be that you don't have much of a sense of smell. Try this: Put your hand over the top of your glass and swirl again. Bring the glass up to your nose. When you release your hand, the wine will smell stronger.

In most cases, you smell subtly pleasant, fruity, even floral wine scents. But watch out for off-odors that tip you to a wine that isn't worth drinking. For example, the wine is going bad if it smells strong, like old sherry. It has *already* gone bad if it smells vinegary. Some wines release too much sulfur and will remind you of rotten eggs. And if the cork went bad, the wine will smell moldy or, as wine experts put it, "mousy."

Take note of any impressions. Is the odor pleasant? Does it smell fruity, or like wood? Let your imagination run rampant. Later, people may discuss the "nose" or "bouquet" of the wine and you will have a chance to say something like: *"This showed lots of butterscotch, ripe peaches, and tropical fruit in the nose,"* or *"It had an intense bouquet of weediness, tobacco, and black currant fruit."*

One last word of warning: Keep your nose out of the wine itself. While there have been no documented drownings from sniffing wine, some people have actually inhaled wine and sneezed it across the room.

3. Sip and slurp.

Finally, the moment of truth: Put the glass to your lips and take a good sip. *But don't swallow yet.*

Swish the wine around your mouth as if using mouthwash. The idea is to cover all your taste buds. Now it gets tricky, so practice this at home to avoid an embarrassing mess. Keeping the wine in your mouth and your teeth tightly clenched, open your mouth slightly and draw in air between your teeth and over your tongue. This draws the wine's vapors deep into your nasal passages, giving you the one-two punch of taste and scent working in harmony.

Try to pick out and compare the mixture of the wine's essential taste components. Is the taste more sweet or bitter? Fruity or "woody"? Smooth or acidic? Wine has scores of chemical compounds in varying combinations that determine its flavor. Is the combined effect pleasant like an orchestra playing together, or discordant like one still tuning up? Take note of your impression of the taste. Much of the answer is completely subjective—in one sense, if you like it, it's good wine. On the other hand, while experts themselves often disagree, there are certain agreed-upon truisms and hallmarks:

- Some acidity is necessary to give the wine "vitality," but not so much that it tastes like a grapefruit.

- Young wines will normally taste "fruitier"—more like fresh fruit—than aged wines. Different reviewers will see that as either a virtue or a sign that the wine needs more aging.

- Sweetness is desirable only in certain, almost always white, wines ... almost never red.

- Tannin, which is responsible for that astringent taste in strong black tea, appears in wine as well, especially red. It provides the flavor backbone of many wines, but shouldn't overpower the other elements.

4. Swallow or spit.

Now you finally get to swallow the wine. Or, if you're tasting a lot of wines, are in a 12-step program, or just want to keep your consciousness clear for some reason, spit the wine discreetly into the cups or plastic buckets provided for that purpose. (It's considered bad form, no matter how discreetly you perform the task, to use other nearby containers such as vases, potted plants, or fish aquariums.)

Concentrate on the aftertaste right after the wine leaves your mouth. It should be, to quote one wine expert, "clean, persistent, and fruity." The duration of the aftertaste (or the "finish," in wine-speak) varies with the type and age of the wine, but generally the longer the better. Take note of the aftertaste, and then cleanse your palate with a cracker and water before going on to the next wine. At the end of the tasting, you'll often have a chance to share your perceptions, so take careful note of the chapters on how to speak wine-speak (see page 78).

HOSTING YOUR OWN TASTING PARTY

A tasting party doesn't need to be elaborate or expensive. It can be a chance to compare a dozen different types of wines, from white to red. Or, if your friends are mostly wannabes, it can be an eye-opener to sample a dozen different brands and years of the same type of wine all at once (a dozen different Zinfandels, for example).

Equipment

- A good corkscrew.
- Glasses. Clear, stemmed, and preferably tulip-shaped. Make sure that they have been well-cleaned and

rinsed to remove any traces of dish detergents. (As mentioned before, some wine appreciators don't *ever* use soaps of any kind when washing their wine glasses.) Purists would insist that each person should have a separate glass for each wine, but if necessary, your guests can rinse and wipe one glass over and over again.

- Spitting cups or buckets.

- Bread or low-salt crackers, and a pitcher of water with (even more) glasses, to cleanse the palate between wines.

- Notepads and pencils for recording impressions.

- And, of course, wines. Half a bottle of each wine is enough for a tasting group of six people.

Set-up

Put a white tablecloth on your table. The white background lets you see the subtle color differences between wines. Put the bottles in brown paper bags marked with a random letter so that your tasters aren't affected by the labels or brand names. Despite what you've seen in less formal urban outdoor wine-tasting groups, passing around the bottle in a paper bag without using glasses is considered a grave *faux pas*.

The Tasting

Uncork the wines and put about a 1/4 cup of wine in each glass. This allows room for your guests to swirl the wine without threatening to make big colorful stains on your tablecloth or carpet.

The Judging

- Decide on a scoring criteria and encourage your guests to jot honest reactions on paper, yet hide their immediate reactions to avoid influencing others.

- How to score the wine? This can be a simple 1–100 numerical rating. For additional fun, encourage your guests to also rate the wines in wine-speak. Give a prize to anybody who can top these genuine reviews by actual wine experts:

  —"A graceful bubbly, one that's creamy and rich, a toasty wine with pear and hazelnut notes that keep singing on the finish."

  —"Smashingly intense, smoky, exotic nose of sweet jammy fruit, new oak and a multitude of spices."

  —"Forward, quite herbaceous nose, showing eucalyptus, tobacco leaf, and smoky oak, but only shy fruit. A stylish wine, with very herbaceous flavors."

—"A silky suppleness, a mellow fruitiness, and a lovely bouquet of cedar, incense, tobacco, and old leather that characterizes mature red wines of real excellence."

—"Appealing nose of spice, cedar, light herbs, chocolate and ripe cassis, with plenty of vanilla oak. Rich, plummy, red currant flavors showing noticeable oak."

(Note: For more hints, see the next chapter on wine-speak.)

• Just for fun, include one of the wines twice. See if the two wines get scored differently. After scoring and discussion, reveal your skullduggery and see if your guests can guess which two bags contain the same wine.

* * *

"If you make your pleasure depend on drinking good wine, you condemn yourself to the pain of sometimes drinking bad wine. We must have a less exacting and freer taste. To be a good drinker, one must not have so delicate a palate."

—Michel de Montaigne,
sixteenth-century French philosopher

Wine-O-Matic:
YOU Can Talk Like an Expert

Tongue-tied at the wine tasting? Don't know what to say about that wine in front of you? Easy. Use this handy guide. Pick a word, any word, and you can sound as knowledgeable as any wine expert. By the way, every descriptive word and phrase below, with the exception of a few obvious jokes, was selected from a genuine, serious wine review. Just goes to show what happens when self-administering a drug is part of your job.

Wine-O-Matic

"This is a(n) *(pick one or more from column A)* wine that is full of *(pick one or more from column B)*."

Column A	Column B
overblown	liveliness
ultra-ripe	youthful exuberance
monster	uncontroversial pleasures
high-extract	plentiful fruit flavors
ripe	silky suppleness
big	mellow fruitiness
shy	jamminess
elegant	acidity
classy	grassiness
bilious	gassiness
restrained	earthiness
forward	lushness
rich	balance
round	structure
bosomy	strength
unobtrusive	character
bold and brassy	unbridled hedonism
viscous	unrelenting intensity
soft	passionate entwinement
complex	eroticism
young and fruity	glass shards
brooding	
generous	
brilliantly flawed	
savagely aggressive	

"The bouquet has touches of *(pick one or more of list below)*. This wine has a medley of *(pick several)* flavors with notes of *(pick one or more)*. It ends with a finish of *(pick one or more)*."

buttered toast	honey	prunes
apple	black cherry	strawberry
citrus	red cherry	cream
pear	Cheez-wiz	French Oak
tropical fruit	sage	mint
cedar	vanilla	cassis fruit
cinnamon	clove	plum
11 secret herbs & spices	melon	buttery
peaches	leather	Kool-Aid
chocolate	butterscotch	currant
Rocky Road	S'Mores	hazelnut
eucalyptus	tobacco	coconut
honeysuckle	skunk cabbage	slate
green apple	mineral	cranberry
flint	cement	cheeseburger
cranapple	Lymon	Lemon Pledge
grapefruit	piney-fresh	banana
cotton	almond	beef jerky
smoked bacon	roast beef	black pepper
cat piss	apricot	wet rock
bell-pepper	Dr. Pepper	sulfur
compost	green olive	barnyard
weeds	grasses	

Do You Need a Wine Cellar?

If you are going to become a virtual wine connoisseur, do you need to have a wine cellar?

But of course, *mon ami*. A wine connoisseur without a wine cellar is like a chef without a stove, or a couch potato without a television. There are four reasons to start storing and aging wine: #1, to experiment with the tastes of the different ages of the same wine, #2, to experience the joy of collecting, #3, to save money (most stores offer a discount on wine by the case), and #4, so you can casually mention it in conversation. "I've got a case of Boone's Farm 1992 in my cellar that is aging quite nicely," you say casually, and except for the minor *faux pas* of mentioning that particular brand name, you have made a superlative impression.

"But," you may object, "I don't have thousands of dollars to sink into a climate-controlled wine room in my basement. Heck, I don't even have a basement."

Don't worry. It doesn't have to be that complicated.

True, there is a lot of mystique about a wine cellar, as well there should be. Wherever you decide to store wine, even if under the house or in a back closet somewhere, it should be out of the way of your normal day to day living. In part that's because wine needs peace and quiet without much shaking or other disturbance. Also when you are serving guests, there's a definite advantage to be gained by announcing casually, "Oh, I've got just the right thing in the cellar," disappearing mysteriously into the bowels of the house, and eventually reappearing, gently wiping a dusty bottle of 1978 Paul Jaboulet Aine Hermitage la Chapelle.

Or, for that matter, even a 1992 Chateau le Boone's Farm looks impressive under the circumstances.

Making Your "Cellar"

As mentioned, you could spend a few thousand dollars on a climate-controlled room. But don't bother. Here's a tip on what you need most: "Treat your wine like a demanding guest who has insomnia," says one expert. "Keep them in a cool dark place where they won't be constantly jarred by household activity."

• Remember this bit of math: Wine + oxygen = vinegar. A dry cork allows air to leak into the bottle. Store bottles on their sides to keep their corks moist.

• That's also one reason to avoid extreme changes in temperature, because heat and cold cause expansion and contraction. If the wine heats up, the pressure inside the bottle will try to push air out of the bottle; if it contracts, it will try to suck air into it.

• Dark. Many wines come in tinted bottles for a reason— excessive light can hurt the wine. Your storage area should be free of bright lights and sunlight.

• Cool, but not cold, allows the best aging. The recommendation is a temperature in the range of fifty-five to sixty degrees ... which, conveniently, is also within the recommended drinking temperature for red wine. But even this rule isn't ironclad. If your "cellar" is warmer, it just means that your wines will age faster; if cooler, they'll age slower. The secret is to avoid extremes. Neither freezing nor spending a lot of time over seventy degrees is going to do your wine any good. Some people use a basement corner away from the furnace. Others use a dark closet on the north side of the house, or, in moderate climates, tuck their wine under the floor in the crawl space above the foundation. Some use an *unplugged* refrigerator or freezer for insulation to slow temperature changes.

• Some experts say the humidity level should be high. Others call that outdated advice from the days when wine was stored in air-permeable wood barrels that allowed a great deal of evaporation. Those who believe in the importance of keeping both ends of the cork damp suggest sixty-five to seventy percent humidity and using racks made of redwood, which is relatively immune to mildew.

• Experts also suggest that "excessive" vibration and movement be avoided. However, they can't seem to agree about how much is excessive. Some think aging wine should be sheltered from street noises, the hums of refrigerators, heaters and air conditioners, or the constant vibration of nearby foot traffic. Others think that these warnings are silly and are more concerned about bottles being constantly jarred in a hallway coat closet or periodically shaken and dropped by small children.

• When you periodically inspect, admire, and fondle your wine bottles lovingly, peel the foil caps off the bottles to keep an eye on the condition of the corks. Look for discoloration or other signs of leakage. If you see anything suspicious, drink that bottle before it goes bad.

Which Wines Age Well?

Of all wine produced, ninety percent is consumed within a year. Some wines are as good as they're ever going to be on the day they're released from the vintner. That's true of many whites. In fact, some whites don't age well at all (only Chardonnay and Riesling, in fact, are considered "long-lived" enough to safely age more than ten years). Others—reds with a moderate amount of tannin, the bitter ingredient in tea that leaches from the wooden barrels—start tasting "supple" and fruity instead of bitter in three to five years. Wines with more tannin require seven to ten years or more to reach a nice mellow balance between the flavor elements.

It all comes down to taste, of course. Which is why "putting down" a good number of bottles of each wine makes sense. It allows you to break open a bottle every few years and see whether the rest of the bottles have mellowed to your tastes. Some suggested guidelines from experts:

- **Cabernet Sauvignon:** seven to ten years
- **Merlot:** three to five years
- **Pinot Noir:** light-colored Pinots, three to five years; darker ones, five to eight
- **Riesling:** seven to ten years
- **Zinfandel:** three to five years
- **Sparkling wines:** three to seven years

One last hint: If you are storing an American wine, try sending a note to the winery where it was made asking their recommendation. Most will get back to you, especially if you send a self-addressed stamped envelope.

Buying Wine to Store

There's an oft-quoted bit of advice that a good bottle of wine shouldn't cost more than a good bottle of scotch. There are plenty of good ten to fifteen dollar bottles of wine that will get substantially better (and, incidentally, more valuable). The more expensive wines are not necessarily better—just charging what the market will bear.

On the other hand, experts advise against buying really cheap wine with the idea that storing it may make it substantially better.

"There are no long shots in buying wine for the cellar," says one. "Bottles that become immensely valuable with passing time were expensive to begin with."

Newsletters

If you want advice on what wines to buy each year, or at least want to find out what everyone else will be buying, subscribe to a wine buyers' guide like the *Wine Advocate* or *Wine Spectator*. If nothing else, you and your friends can have fun mocking the overblown wine descriptions (*"this savagely aggressive Pinot, full of unbridled yet unassuming passion ... "*). Doing so is especially rewarding over a bottle of 1991 Boone's Farm, served the way God and the Gallo Brothers intended—outside, from a brown paper bag.

AGING THROUGH THE AGES

The idea of aging some wines to bring out mellow flavors is a relatively new invention (well, in the last four or five centuries anyway). Before that, the idea was to simply to make wine that wouldn't turn to vinegar before the next harvest.

Once they got the idea, winemakers tried a variety of aging techniques. By the second half of the eighteenth century, the British were shipping barrels of Madeira as ballast to the West Indies and back because they had accidentally discovered that the constant rocking, salt water, and stifling heat somehow gave the wine a "softness and depth of flavor."

Other winemakers swore that you could smooth out the flavor of wine by burying the bottles for six months in pits filled with horse manure.

Eventually, it became clear that it was the heat that was important, not the horse manure or the rocking in bilge water. Winemakers came up with a wine lodge equipped with a huge stove and water pipes to circulate the heat around the wine barrels.

The Bard Meets Colombard:
Shakespeare on Wine

William Shakespeare vinted words with a wit that was as dry and sweet as any wine. So it's not surprising that, in his plays, he expressed a few opinions on the subject.

"O thou invisible spirit of wine! if thou hast no name to be known by, let us call thee devil!"—*Othello*

"Come, come; good wine is a good familiar creature if it be well used; exclaim no more against it."—*Othello*

"A good sherris-sack hath a two-fold operation in it. It ascends me into the brain, dries me there all the foolish and crudy vapours which environ it, makes it apprehensive, quick, forgetful, full of nimble, fiery, and delectable shapes, which delivered o'er the voice, the tongue, which is the birth, becomes excellent wit. The second property of your excellent sherris is the warming of the blood, which (cold and settled) left the liver white and pale, which is the badge of pusillanimity and cowardice, but the sherris warms it and makes it course from the inwards to the parts extreme. . . . If I had a thousand sons, the first humane principle I would teach them should be to forswear thin potations, and to addict themselves to sack."—*Henry IV*

"A man cannot make him laugh; but that's no marvel; he drinks no wine."—*Henry IV*

"I pray you, do not fall in love with me,
For I am falser than vows made in wine."

—*As You Like It*

Wine and Health

"Wherever wine is lacking, drugs become necessary."
—*The Talmud*

Another reason to drink wine in moderation is that doing so seems to have some health benefits. Still the debate goes on: Is wine a medicinal elixir, a dangerous drug . . . or both? It depends on who you ask.

Using wine as medicine goes back into prehistory. Doctors through time have tried to research and codify its use. In ancient Egypt, wine was mixed with honey and recommended as a cure-all medicine and enema to "regulate the urine, cause purgation, kill tapeworm, and relieve anorexia, insomnia, and all diseases marked by cough." Arnaldus de Villanova, in the first known wine book, *Liber de Vinis,* in 1311 prescribed exotic and flavored wines for every sort of ailment including ox-tongue wine for healing the insane and rosemary wine for stimulating your soul, keeping you young, improving your facial beauty, and cleaning your teeth. In 1892, physicians in Paris and Austria found that wine, even in diluted form, killed cholera and typhoid bacteria and that wine drinkers were statistically less likely to be stricken during a cholera epidemic.

In our time, the research on wine and alcohol has been mixed enough that you can find supporting evidence for any point of view you wish to support, whether you believe that wine is an addictive poison, a mild yet beneficial relaxant, or a potent medicine.

The Bad News

First, wine's dark side. Wine, taken regularly by certain people can lead to addiction. Heavy drinking, especially in combination with smoking, leads to liver damage including scarring (cirrhosis). Alcohol can cause birth defects, according to several studies, and it apparently can also pass into breast milk, according to researchers in Philadelphia. Also, alcohol can combine badly, even fatally, with prescription and other drugs. Wine in large amounts—three drinks or more a day—may increase the incidence of strokes, according to a study by Kaiser Permanente Medical Center in California. And even one drink of wine can temporarily increase blood pressure, according to the Alcohol Research Group in Berkeley, California.

Because red wine soaks in the grape skins for a long time, it may contain traces of dozens of dangerous insecticides, fungicides, and herbicides, according to the Center for Science in the Public Interest. The group lists sulfites and eighty other additives routinely used in wine production, "including acids, bases, sugars, plastics, and a wide range of animal products." Red wine may also be one of the substances like monosodium glutamate, chocolate, and cheese that trigger migraine headaches, according to an Italian headache specialist. (However, the effect might also be psychosomatic— a University of California-Davis researcher found that subjects who complained about getting headaches from red wine also got them from drinking colored water placebos.)

Wine and Health

The Good News

On the other hand, the medical community recognizes that wine has benefits, too. For example, many hospitals and rest homes now routinely serve wine for its relaxation, social, sleep-inducing, and anti-depressant properties. Wine in moderation reduces harmful stress, according to research at the University of California-Davis.

According to a ten-year study of 4,000 residents of Alameda, California, people who drank 1–2 drinks a day had a lower mortality rate than heavier drinkers or even non-drinkers. Red wine contains quercetin, which is one of the strongest anti-cancer agents known, according to a University of California researcher. American and British doctors report that nonsmokers who consumed alcohol in moderation are 65% to 85% percent more resistant to five strains of common cold viruses than nondrinkers.

There may be particularly hopeful news about wine's effects on cardiovascular problems. A forty-year study of the citizens of Framingham, Massachusetts, indicates that red wine reduces the level of "bad" LDL cholesterol and inhibits its oxidation, reducing the accumulation of cholesterol on artery walls. Adding low-fat icing to the reduced-calorie cake, researchers at Harvard say that wine also apparently increases "good" HDL cholesterol. Beer and red wine—but not white wine—act as an anti-clotting agent, according to researchers at the University of Wisconsin. Forty-five minutes after drinking a glass of red wine, the tendency of blood platelets to form clots was reduced by 39%, which can be good news since blood clots in the arteries are a major factor in heart attacks.

"The French Paradox"—the much-heralded discovery of

a Boston University School of Medicine researcher that indicated that patè-gulping French folks had a lower average cholesterol level than Americans—may be evidence of the cardiovascular benefits of red wine. Or it may not. Later studies, not so widely heralded, indicate that the French have only recently been affluent enough to partake regularly in fatty foods and as a result that they may be moving toward a similar heart attack rate as *le Americains*.

Wine:
Just What the Doctor Ordered?

"Drink no longer water but use a little wine for thy stomach's sake."—1st Timothy 5:23

"Wine is the . . . invigorator of mind and body, antidote to sleeplessness, sorrow, and fatigue . . . producer of hunger, happiness, and digestion."—Indian medical text, sixth century B.C.

"Soft dark wines are moister, they are flatulent and pass better by stool. . . . Harsh white wines heat without drying, and they pass better by urine than by stool. New wines pass by stool better than other wines because they are nearer the must, and more nourishing. . . . Must causes wind, disturbs the bowels and empties them. . . . Sweet wine causes less heaviness in the head than fully fermented wine, goes to the brain less, evacuates the bowels more than the other, but causes swelling of the spleen and liver. . . . It passes more readily into the bladder, being diuretic and laxative, it always is in many ways beneficial in acute diseases. . . . Should you suspect, however, in these diseases an overpowering heaviness of the head, or that the brain is affected, there must be total abstinence from wine."—Hippocrates, 420 B.C.

"It is well known among physicians that the best of the nourishing foods is one that the Muslim religion forbids—that is, wine.... It is rapidly digested and helps to digest other foods.... The benefits of wine are many if it is taken in the proper amount, as it keeps the body in a healthy condition and cures many illnesses."—Maimonides, personal doctor to the Sultan Saldin, twelfth century

"Take especial care that thou delight not in wine, for there never was any man that came to honour or preferment that loved it; for it transformeth a man into a beast, decayeth the health, poisoneth the breath, destroyeth the natural heat, brings a man's stomach to an artificial heat, deformeth the face, rotteth the teeth, and to conclude, maketh a man contemptible, soon old, and despised of all wise and worthy men, hated in thy servants, in thyself and companions, for it is a bewitching and infectious vice."—Sir Walter Raleigh, best known for introducing that beneficial herb tobacco to Europe

"Claret is recommended ... particularly for children, for literary persons, and for all those whose occupations are chiefly carried on indoors, and which tax the brain more than the muscles."—Dr. Robert Druitt, 1860

"Wine is the most hygienic of all beverages."—Louis Pasteur

"Drink a glass of wine after your soup and steal a ruble from your doctor."—Russian proverb